Mike McGrath

Excel VBA

Second Edition

In easy steps is an imprint of In Easy Steps Limited
16 Hamilton Terrace · Holly Walk · Leamington Spa
Warwickshire · United Kingdom · CV32 4LY
www.ineasysteps.com

Second Edition

Notice of Liability
Every effort has been made to ensure that this book contains accurate
and current information. However, In Easy Steps Limited and the
author shall not be liable for any loss or damage suffered by readers
as a result of any information contained herein.

Trademarks
Microsoft®, Windows® and Excel® are registered trademarks of
Microsoft Corporation. All other trademarks are acknowledged as
belonging to their respective companies.

In Easy Steps Limited supports The Forest Stewardship Council (FSC),
the leading international forest certification organization. All our titles
that are printed on Greenpeace approved FSC certified paper carry the
FSC logo.

MIX
Paper from
responsible sources
FSC® C020837

FSC
www.fsc.org

Printed and bound in the United Kingdom

ISBN 978-1-84078-737-5

Contents

1 Getting started

Welcome to the exciting
world of Excel VBA (Visual
Basic for Applications). This
chapter demonstrates how
to create a VBA macro for
Excel workbooks.

Introducing Excel VBA

Visual Basic for Applications (VBA) is the programming language that is built into the Excel spreadsheet application and other Microsoft Office applications. It extends Excel so it can perform tasks that can't be done with standard Excel tools, and provides the capability to automate many routine tasks.

The examples in this book assume the reader is an experienced Excel user who can accomplish these fundamental operations:

- Create workbooks and insert worksheets

- Navigate around a workbook and worksheet

- Use the Excel Ribbon interface

- Name cells and ranges

- Use the Excel worksheet functions

All examples are demonstrated using Excel 2016, although most examples are also applicable to earlier versions of Excel.

Enabling VBA

Before you can get started using the capabilities of VBA, it must first be enabled in your Excel installation:

If you're just starting out with Excel, please refer to our companion book **Excel 2016 in easy steps**.

1 Launch Excel, then choose to open a **Blank workbook**

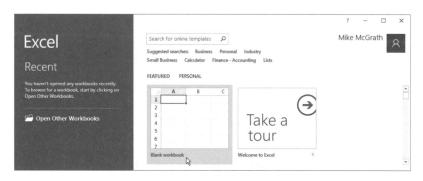

All the examples in this book are available for free download at **www.ineasysteps. com/resource-centre/ downloads**

2 When the workbook opens, choose the **File** tab on the Excel Ribbon

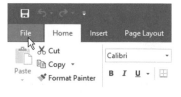

3 Next, select the **Options** item – to open the "Excel Options" dialog box

4 In the Excel Options dialog, choose the **Customize Ribbon** item on the left-hand pane

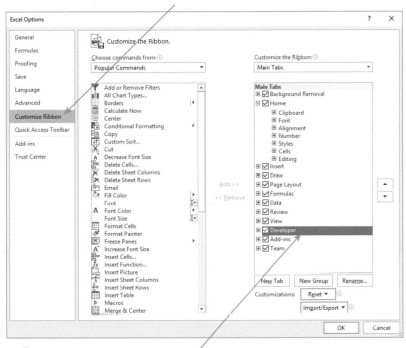

You can also open the Excel Options dialog box by pressing the **Alt** + **F** + **T** keys.

5 Now, check the **Developer** option box in the right-hand pane

6 Click the **OK** button to apply the change and to close the Excel Options dialog box

In the Excel Options dialog you can click the **+** button beside the **Developer** item to reveal the groups it contains. If you right-click on any group, a context menu offers you options to modify the groups that will appear on the Developer tab.

7 See that a **Developer** tab has been added to the Ribbon

8 Choose the Developer tab to see a **Visual Basic** button in the Ribbon's "Code" group – VBA is now enabled

Recording a macro

Having enabled VBA, as described on pages 8-9, you can create a simple app by recording a "macro" to store actions:

1 Open a blank workbook in Excel, then select worksheet cell **A1**

2 On the Developer tab, click the **Record Macro** button in the Code group to launch the "Record Macro" dialog box

3 Type a name of your choice in the dialog's **Macro name** field – for example, type "BookTitle"

4 Next, type a letter in the dialog's **Shortcut key** field – for example, type "T", to create a **Ctrl + Shift + T** shortcut

5 Now, choose to store the macro in **This Workbook**

6 Click the **OK** button to close the Record Macro dialog, and to begin recording actions

7 Type the title of this book into previously selected cell A1, then hit **Enter** – to enter the title text into the cell

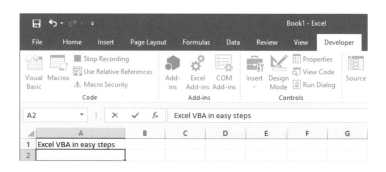

8 Notice that focus has moved, so cell A2 is now automatically selected after you hit the **Enter** key

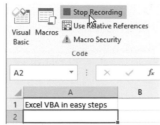

The **Record Macro** button changes to **Stop Recording** when recording is taking place.

9 Now, click the **Stop Recording** button in the Code group on the Developer tab – to stop recording your actions

10 Click the **Macros** button in the Code group to launch the "Macro" dialog box and choose to see macros in **This Workbook**

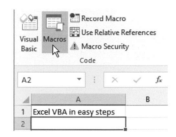

11 Select the "BookTitle" macro, then click the **Run** button to execute the macro and see the book title text appear in the automatically selected cell **A2**

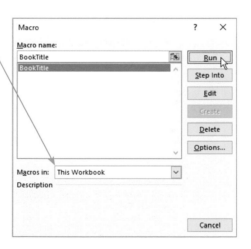

You can also use the shortcut keys **Alt** + **F8** to open the Macros dialog at any time.

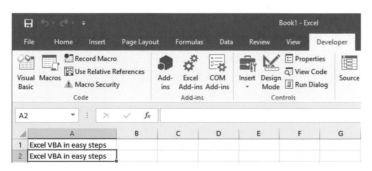

Viewing macro code

Having created a macro, as described on the previous page, the VBA programming instructions that were written when the macro was created can be viewed in the Visual Basic Editor:

1 On Excel's Developer tab, click the **Visual Basic** button in the Code group – to launch the Visual Basic Editor

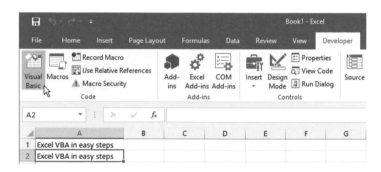

2 In the Visual Basic Editor, select **View**, **Project Explorer** – to open the "Project Explorer" window

12

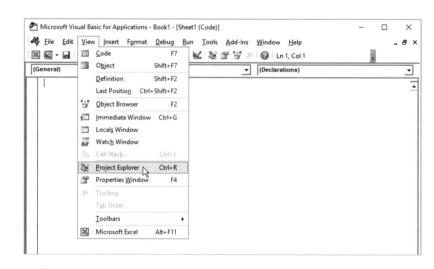

3 In Project Explorer, click the + button beside the **Book1** project to expand its contents

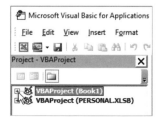

4 Now, in Project Explorer, double-click the **Module1** node within the "Modules" folder – to see the macro VBA code

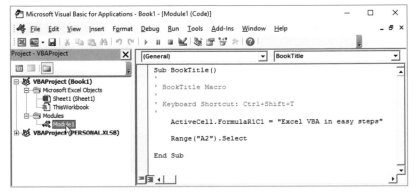

The other project seen in this Project Explorer window is a special **PERSONAL.XLSB** workbook in which macros can be saved on your computer. This will not appear in the Project Explorer window until a macro has been saved in it – as demonstrated on page 19.

Code analysis

- **Sub BookTitle ( )** – This declares the beginning of a "subroutine" (**Sub**) with the same name you gave to the macro (**BookTitle**) and was written when it began recording.

- ' **BookTitle Macro** – This is a comment, confirming that this subroutine is for a macro of your chosen name.

- ' **Keyboard Shortcut: Ctrl+Shift+T** – This is another comment, describing the shortcut keys you chose to run this macro.

- **ActiveCell.FormulaR1C1 = "Excel VBA in easy steps"** – This is an instruction, that was written when you typed the book title into the cell and hit the **Enter** key.

- **Range("A2").Select** – This is an instruction, that was written as focus moved to cell A2 after you hit the **Enter** key.

- **End Sub** – This denotes the end of this macro subroutine, and was written when you stopped recording.

The color used in the code is the default syntax highlighting that the Visual Basic Editor automatically applies for easier reading. Blue is applied to "keywords" that have special meaning in Visual Basic code, and green is applied to comments describing the code. For clarity, the same color syntax highlighting is also used in the example code listed in the steps provided throughout this book.

The **( )** parentheses that appear in the first line of code can contain a parameter list. This is demonstrated later, on page 90.

All lines that begin with an apostrophe are simply ignored when the macro is executed.

Testing a macro

Before starting to record the macro, as described on page 10, shortcut keys were specified in the Record Macro dialog and these can now be tested to ensure they can run the macro:

1 With the Visual Basic Editor open, select **View, Microsoft Excel**, or click the ⊠ button on the toolbar to return to the Excel interface

Hot tip

You can use the shortcut keys **Alt** + **F11** to close the Visual Basic Editor.

2 Next, select empty cell **A3**

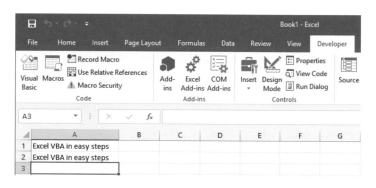

3 Now, press the **Ctrl** + **Shift** + **T** shortcut keys to test run the macro – the book title should appear in the cell you selected and the focus returned to cell **A2** as instructed in code

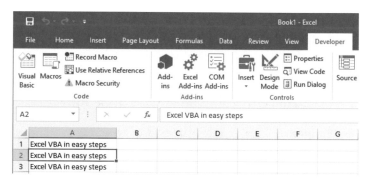

Hot tip

If you try to specify a shortcut key that is already designated for use by another macro in the same workbook, a dialog will appear requesting you to specify an alternative shortcut key – so you cannot accidentally duplicate.

14

It is important to remember that cell A1 was selected before the macro recording began, otherwise the action of selecting that cell would be written as an instruction in the macro. This would mean the book title could only be written into cell A1 each time the macro was run.

Editing macro code

Now you are sure the macro can be run by both the Run button in the Macro dialog, and by the Ctrl + Shift + T shortcut keys you specified, but you probably will not need it to return focus to cell A2 after each run. The code can be edited to remove the instruction to return focus, and also to style the text it writes:

1 On Excel's Developer tab, click the **Visual Basic** button in the Code group to launch the Visual Basic Editor

2 In Project Explorer, double-click the project's **Module1** item to see the macro VBA code

3 Next, delete this instruction line that returns focus
Range("A2").Select

4 Now, add these instructions anywhere within the subroutine to style the text in bold red
ActiveCell.Font.Bold = True
ActiveCell.Font.Color = vbRed

The macro
VBA code
should now
look something
like this:

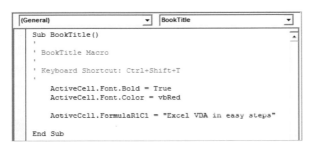

```
(General)                          ▼  BookTitle                      ▼
Sub BookTitle()
'
' BookTitle Macro
'
' Keyboard Shortcut: Ctrl+Shift+T
'
    ActiveCell.Font.Bold = True
    ActiveCell.Font.Color = vbRed

    ActiveCell.FormulaR1C1 = "Excel VBA in easy steps"

End Sub
```

5 Return to Excel, then select any cell and press the **Ctrl** + **Shift** + **T** shortcut keys to run this edited macro

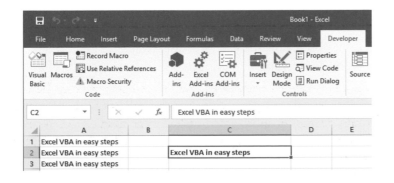

Hot tip

As you type instructions a pop-up box will often appear when you type a period, to offer a list of suggestions from which you can choose an item.

Hot tip

The eight Visual Basic color constants are **vbRed**, **vbGreen**, **vbBlue**, **vbYellow**, **vbMagenta**, **vbCyan**, **vbBlack**, and **vbWhite** – see page 53 for more on constants.

Don't forget

Although the lines of VBA code are executed from top to bottom, their order is unimportant in this macro – the cell's styling can be set before or after its content is added.

Hot tip

Macros recorded using relative referencing are often more flexible, as they can be applied anywhere in a workbook.

Referencing relatives

Excel has two macro recording modes that differ in the way they refer to cells on the worksheet. The default recording mode, used in the previous examples, refers to cells by their "absolute" position on the worksheet – cell A1, A2, A3, and so on. The alternative recording mode refers to cell locations by their position on the worksheet "relative" to other cells – offset by a specified number of rows and columns from another cell. The difference between the two recording modes is important, as macros that use absolute referencing always reference the same cell locations regardless of the currently selected cell, whereas macros that use relative referencing reference cells at locations offset from the selected cell:

1. Clear all worksheet cells, then select cell **A1** and begin a macro named "AbsoluteBookTitle"

2. Type this book's topic, then select cell **B2** and type this book's series name

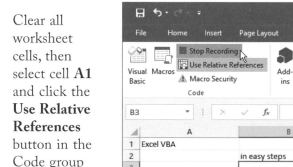

3. Hit **Enter**, then click **Stop Recording**

4. Clear all worksheet cells, then select cell **A1** and click the **Use Relative References** button in the Code group

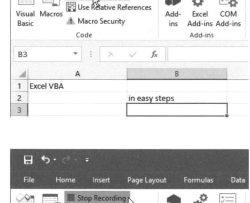

Don't forget

Shortcut keys might also be specified to run these macros. For example, **Ctrl + Shift + A** (Absolute) and **Ctrl + Shift + R** (Relative).

5. Begin a macro named "RelativeBookTitle", then repeat Steps 2 and 3 to complete the macro

...cont'd

6 Click the **Visual Basic** button to open the Visual Basic Editor, then compare the VBA code of each macro

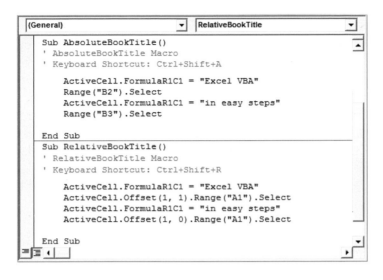

Hot tip

Empty comment lines are removed from this screenshot to save space.

When selecting cell B2, absolute referencing refers to it by name, but relative referencing refers to it as offset by 1 row and 1 column from the initially selected cell. To compare performance:

7 Clear all cells, then select cell **A2** and run the macro named "AbsoluteBookTitle"

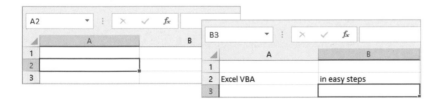

8 Again, clear all cells, then once more select cell **A2** and run the macro named "RelativeBookTitle"

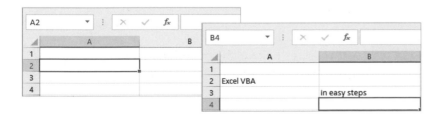

Hot tip

In this example, the macro using absolute referencing writes the book series name in the cell named **B2**, whereas the macro using relative referencing writes the book series name in cell **B3** – as it is offset by 1 row and 1 column from the initially selected cell.

Saving macros

Since Excel 2007, workbook files have had the standard file extension of ".xlsx", but these cannot contain Visual Basic macros. In order to save an Excel workbook and its macros, it must instead be saved as an Excel Macro-Enabled Workbook that is given a file extension of ".xlsm". If you save a workbook containing a macro as a standard ".xlsx" file, all macro code will be lost – but Excel will warn you before this happens:

Don't forget

Choose a folder location where you want to save workbooks. Here, it's a folder named "Excel Workbooks" within the system's **Documents** folder.

1 In Excel, select **File**, **Save As**, then type "BookTitle" as the workbook name and click the **Save** button

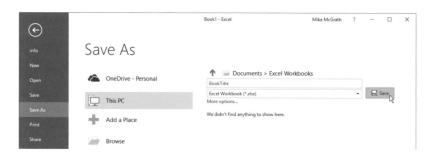

2 If the workbook contains a macro, a warning dialog will appear asking if you wish to proceed – unless you want to save the workbook without its macro, click the **No** button

Hot tip

Click the ▼ button to reveal a drop-down list of file types from which to choose.

3 Change the file type to Excel Macro-Enabled Workbook, then click the **Save** button to save the complete workbook

...cont'd

Although most macros are intended for use in a specific workbook, general-purpose macros that may be useful in many workbooks can be saved in the special Personal Macro Workbook. This is a file named "personal.xlsb" that automatically opens in the background when Excel starts up – so the macros it contains are available to any other workbook. To save a macro in the Personal Macro Workbook, simply choose that option in the Record Macro dialog before you begin recording a macro:

1 Click the **Record Macro** button and call the macro "Name", then choose the **Personal Macro Workbook** option

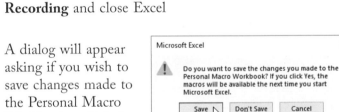

2 Type your name into the selected cell, then select **Stop Recording** and close Excel

3 A dialog will appear asking if you wish to save changes made to the Personal Macro Workbook – click the **Save** button to retain the macro

4 Next, start Excel and begin a new **Blank workbook**, then click the **Macros** button in the Code group

5 Now, choose the saved "Name" macro and click **Run** to write your name into a cell

The Personal Macro Workbook runs in a hidden window that you can reveal by selecting the **View** tab, then choosing **Unhide** in the Window group.

Confusingly, the dialog says "If you click Yes..." but the button is labeled "Save".

Trusting macros

Excel Workbook files (.xlsx) are regarded as safe, as they merely contain data, whereas Excel Macro-Enabled Workbook files (.xlsm) may pose a potential threat, as they are executable. Recognizing this, Excel automatically disables the macros in an Excel Macro-Enabled Workbook until the user consents to trust their safety. On opening a workbook that contains macros, a security warning offers the user the option to enable macros. If the user consents to enable macros, the workbook is regarded as trustworthy and the security warning will never appear again.

As an alternative to enabling macros in individual workbooks, a folder can be nominated as a trusted location. This then allows Excel Macro-Enabled Workbook files to be placed inside that folder and run without security restrictions:

Hot tip

Both **.xlsx** and **.xlsm** file types store workbook data in XML format. Excel also supports **.xlsb** files that store workbook data in binary format. This is favored by some users, but workbook content is more accessible to other software when stored as XML data.

1 Navigate to the folder containing an Excel Macro-Enabled Workbook, and open it in Excel

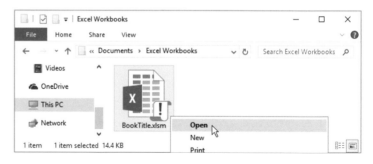

2 Click the **Enable Content** button if you consent to permanently enable macros in this workbook

Beware

Macros have been used to distribute malware – be wary of enabling macros in a workbook from an unknown source.

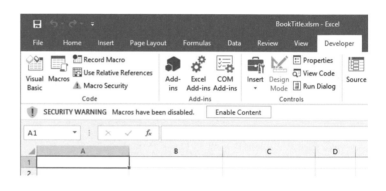

...cont'd

3 Next, click the **Macro Security** button in the Code group to open the "Trust Center" dialog box

4 In the Trust Center dialog, select the **Trusted Locations** item in the left-hand panel

5 Now, click the **Add new location** button to open the "Microsoft Office Trusted Location" dialog

You can also use **Trusted Documents** to nominate a workbook so it will run without security restrictions.

6 Browse to select the folder you wish to nominate as a trusted location for Excel Macro-Enabled Workbooks

7 Click the **OK** button to see your nominated folder added to the list of **Trusted Locations** in the Trust Center

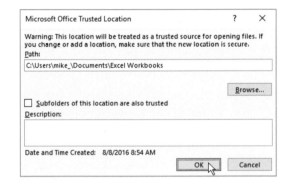

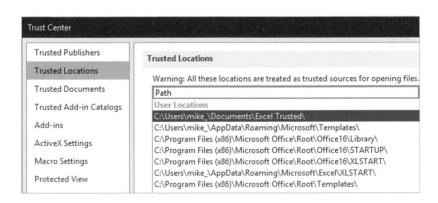

All workbooks in **Trusted Locations** will run without security restrictions.

Summary

- **VBA** (Visual Basic for Applications) is the programming language built into Excel that extends its capabilities beyond the standard Excel tools.

- The Excel Developer option enables VBA and adds a **Developer** tab to the Excel Ribbon.

- The **Code** group on the Developer tab contains a **Record Macro** button with which to create VBA macros.

- The **Macros** button in the Code group lists available macros.

- The **Visual Basic** button in the Code group opens the Visual Basic Editor to inspect macro programming instructions.

- Macro subroutines are stored in a project's **Module1** node.

- Subroutines contain programming instructions and comments.

- Specified shortcut keys, or the **Run** button in the **Macro** dialog, can be used to run a macro.

- Recorded macro programming instructions can be edited in the **Visual Basic Editor** to change the macro's behavior.

- Excel's default macro recording mode references cells by their absolute position.

- The **Use Relative References** button in the Code group enables Excel's alternative macro recording mode, which references cells by their relative position.

- A workbook that contains macro code must be saved as an **Excel Macro-Enabled Workbook** and ".xlsm" file extension.

- General-purpose macros can be saved in the **Personal Macro Workbook** so they are available in other workbooks.

- Excel automatically disables macros in an Excel Macro-Enabled Workbook until the user consents to trust them.

- A folder can be nominated as a **Trusted Location** where Excel Macro-Enabled Workbooks can be placed and run without security restrictions.

2 Writing macros

This chapter demonstrates how to write your own VBA macro instructions and how to reference workbooks, worksheets, and cells.

Exploring the Editor

Hot tip

You can also press **Alt** + **F11** to bring up the Visual Basic Editor.

The Visual Basic Editor is an application that launches in the background when Excel starts up. It is brought to the foreground when the Visual Basic button is clicked in the Developer tab's Code group on the Excel Ribbon. The Visual Basic Editor has several component windows that can be rearranged, opened, and closed. The most useful component windows and convenient arrangement is illustrated below, together with identifying labels:

Menu bar

Toolbar

Project Explorer

Code Window

Properties Window

Immediate Window

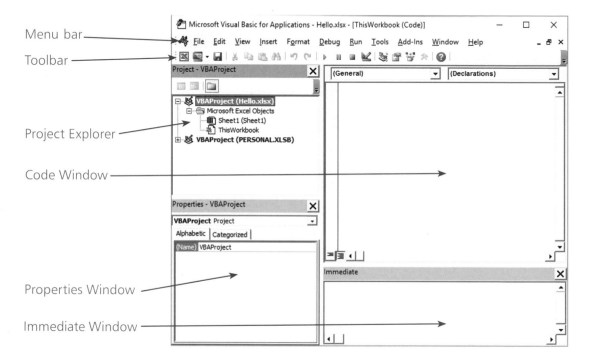

Hot tip

Dotted guidelines appear as you drag the windows to indicate how they will dock into the main Visual Basic Editor frame.

The Code Window will be empty until a VBA code node is selected in Project Explorer. If the other windows are not visible:

1 Select **View, Project Explorer** or press **Ctrl + R**

2 Select **View, Properties Window** or press **F4**

3 Select **View, Immediate Window** or press **Ctrl + G**

4 Click the title bar of each window and drag them until they dock into the arrangement illustrated above

Visual Basic Editor components

- **Menu bar** – provides commands to create, format, run, and debug VBA macros. Many of the commands have keyboard shortcuts, which are listed on the menus.

- **Toolbar** – provides Standard toolbar buttons that offer an alternative one-click option for many commands. There are also Debug, Edit, and UserForm toolbars. Each toolbar can be customized to contain your preferred selection of buttons.

- **Project Explorer** – provides a list of all workbooks currently open in Excel, and displays a tree view of contents within a selected project. The tree view can be expanded by selecting the ⊞ buttons or collapsed by selecting the ⊟ buttons. Each project has a Microsoft Excel Objects folder that contains a workbook object node and an object node for each sheet in that workbook. If the workbook contains macros, there is also a Modules folder that contains module object nodes.

- **Code window** – provides the code content of any module item that is selected in Project Explorer. This is where programming instruction code can be written to create executable macros, or edited to change a macro's behavior.

- **Properties window** – provides an editable list of all properties of the currently selected item. Tabs offer Alphabetic and Categorized arrangements of the list to help you easily find any particular property. Changing any value in the list will change the behavior of that property.

- **Immediate window** – provides direct interaction with the Visual Basic engine. Programming instruction code can be written here and executed immediately. This is most useful to test instructions and debug code.

There are several other windows for more advanced use in addition to the common windows illustrated and described here. These can include Object Browser, Locals Window, and Watch Window. You can explore these via the View menu, but the common windows shown here are all that's needed in most cases. Click the X button at the top right corner of any window to remove it from view in the Visual Basic Editor.

Select **View**, **Toolbars** to explore the additional toolbars that can be added to the Visual Basic Editor.

Type any valid VBA code into the Immediate Window, then hit **Enter** to execute that code. Try executing **MsgBox "Hi!"**.

Creating a macro

When recording macros, if you chose to store the macro in This Workbook, a "Modules" folder is automatically added to the project containing a "Module1" object node – into which the VBA programming instructions are automatically written. When creating your own macro, by manually writing the programming instructions, a new VBA module must first be manually added to the project using the Visual Basic Editor. You can then write these three types of code into the module using the Code Window:

- **Declarations** – statements that provide information for use throughout the module.

- **Subroutines** – programming instructions that perform actions within the workbook when called.

- **Functions** – programming instructions that provide utility by returning a single value to the caller.

One single VBA module can contain multiple declarations, subroutines, and functions, so that all code is stored together. Alternatively, for larger projects, the code may be stored in several modules for convenience – the macro's performance is unaffected:

Hot tip

Subroutines are just like those automatically written when recording a macro. (Declarations and Functions are demonstrated in later chapters.)

26

Hello.xlsm

Hot tip

Alternatively, you can right-click the project name in Project Explorer then select **Insert**, **Module** from the context menu to add a module.

1 Click the **Visual Basic** button in the Developer tab's Code group – to open the Visual Basic Editor

2 In **Project Explorer**, select the project name

3 Next, select **Insert**, **Module** on the Visual Basic Editor menu bar

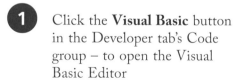

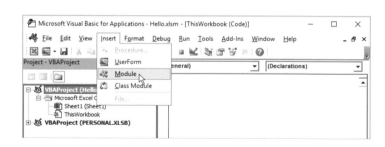

4 In **Project Explorer**, see that a "Modules" folder has been added to this project

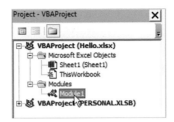

5 Expand the Modules folder, then double-click on the **Module1** object node to open it in the Code Window

6 In the Code Window, type this code then hit **Enter**
Sub Hello ( )

7 See that the cursor is now placed on the line below and an **End Sub** line is automatically written beneath it –

ready to type your code into the subroutine

8 Now, precisely type this line of code
MsgBox "Hello World!" , vbExclamation

9 Click the ▶ Run button, or select **Run**, **Run Sub**, or press **F5**, to execute the macro you have written

10 Click the **OK** button to close the message box, then save the project as an **Excel Macro-Enabled Workbook** (.xlsm)

27

Adding toolbar buttons

Macros that you may want to use often can be conveniently assigned to buttons added to Excel's Quick Access Toolbar:

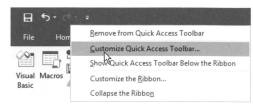

1 Right-click on the Quick Access Toolbar, then choose **Customize Quick Access Toolbar...** from the context menu – to open the Excel Options dialog

2 In the Excel Options dialog, select **Quick Access Toolbar** in the left pane

3 Next, open the "Choose commands from" drop-down list and choose **Macros**

BookTitle.xlsm

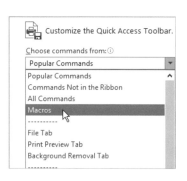

4 Now, select the macro you want to assign to a button

Hot tip

You can also add buttons for commands you frequently use.

28

Hot tip

You can add buttons for macros saved in this workbook or in the Personal Macro Workbook.

5 Then, click the **Add** button to see the selected macro added to the right-hand column

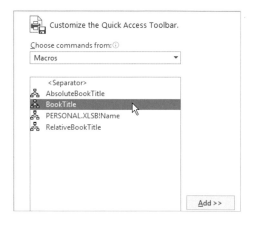

...cont'd

6 Click the **Modify** button below the right-hand column to open the Modify Button dialog

Symbols will not appear in color on the Quick Access Toolbar.

7 In the Modify Button dialog, select a suitable **Symbol**, then click **OK** to see it now appear in the right-hand column

8 In the Excel Options dialog, click the **OK** button to close that dialog and see the button is now added to the Quick Access Toolbar

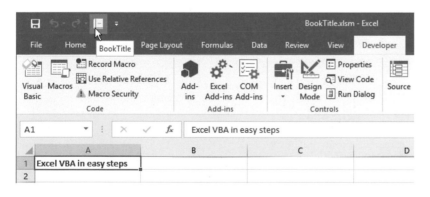

To remove a Quick Access Toolbar button, simply right-click on it then choose **Remove from Quick Access Toolbar**.

9 Click the newly added button to run its assigned macro

Adding form controls

Excel provides a variety of graphical interface components that are known as "form controls". These can be added to a worksheet so the user can easily interact with its content. The most common form control is a button, to which a macro can be assigned:

1 Start a new blank worksheet, then open the **Visual Basic Editor** and add a module to the project

2 Select **Module1** in Project Explorer, then type this code in the Code Window to create a macro named "DateTime" that calls a built-in VBA function to display a message
```
Sub DateTime ( )
MsgBox Now
End Sub
```

Hot tip

There are both standard **Form Controls**, which are designed for worksheets, and similar-looking **ActiveX Controls**, which are typically used on Excel UserForm dialogs (introduced in Chapter 10). Use standard **Form Controls** to place components on a worksheet, for simplicity.

3 Return to Excel and select the **Insert** item in the Controls group on the Developer tab – to see all available controls

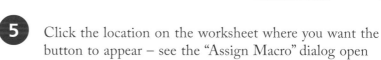

4 Choose the Button control at the top left of the **Form Controls** section

5 Click the location on the worksheet where you want the button to appear – see the "Assign Macro" dialog open

6 Select the "DateTime" macro from **This Workbook**

7 Click **OK** to assign the macro to the button and close the dialog

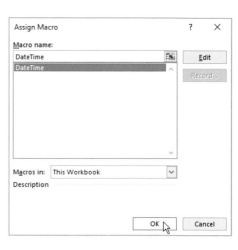

30

8 See four circular "grab handles" appear on the worksheet at the location you chose

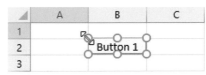

9 Drag the grab handles to resize the button to your preference

10 Next, right-click on the button and choose the **Edit Text** option from the context menu that appears

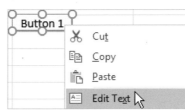

11 See the cursor appear on the button face and change its text to "DateTime"

12 Select any other cell to apply the change, then click the worksheet button to run the macro

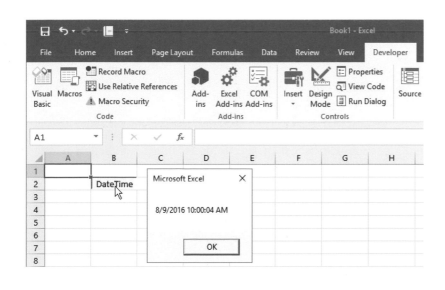

There is also an option on the context menu to **Format Control** where you can change the button's appearance, but it is usually better to stay with the familiar standard appearance that users are accustomed to.

Beware

31

To remove a Form Controls button simply select it then hit the **Delete** key.

Don't forget

Recognizing hierarchy

Application
Workbook
Worksheet
Range
Cell

Objects

Every item in the real world can be described as an "object" and can be seen to be in a hierarchical relationship with other objects. For example, your house is an object. Inside are rooms, which are also objects. Inside the rooms may be furniture objects, and so on.

If you open the Visual Basic Editor and expand any project, you will see it has a Microsoft Excel <u>Objects</u> folder. This is because everything in Excel is an object, within a hierarchical relationship.

In Excel, the **Application** object is the top-level object within the hierarchy, much like your house in the earlier hierarchy. Inside the **Application** object is a workbook object, containing a worksheet object, which in turn contains a range object. In VBA code, you can reference any object within the hierarchy by traversing its levels. For example, you can select cell A1 on "Sheet1" like this:

Application.ThisWorkbook.Sheets("Sheet1").Range("A1").Select

Here, **ThisWorkbook** supplies the workbook object level and **Sheets("Sheet1")** supplies the worksheet object level of the hierarchy. Thankfully, you do not usually need to state all levels of the hierarchy because Excel automatically assumes you are referring to the **Application**, currently active workbook, and currently active worksheet, so you can select cell A1 like this:

Range("A1").Select

Collections

Just as your street may contain a collection of houses, many Excel objects contain collections. For instance, each workbook object contains a collection of worksheets. Each worksheet is given an index number describing its position within the collection, just as a house might have a street number. In VBA code, you can reference any worksheet by specifying its index number, or name, to a **Worksheets( )** method. For example, you can select cell A1 in a worksheet named "Sheet1" using either of these statements:

Worksheets(1).Range("A1").Select

Worksheets("Sheet1").Range("A1").Select

Hot tip

The terms "function" and "method" are somewhat interchangeable, as both provide functionality. Technically speaking, a method is a function that is associated with an object – whereas a function is independent.

Properties

Features of an object are known as its "properties". Properties of your house include its color and its age. Some properties can be changed, such as the color of your house, while other properties are fixed, such as the year your house was built.

Similarly, in Excel, some object properties can be changed, while others are fixed. In VBA code, you reference the property by its name and can assign values to changeable properties. For example, you could rename a worksheet by assigning a new value to its changeable **Name** property, like this:

Worksheets("Sheet1").Name = "DataSheet"

Conversely, you could display the content of cell A1 by referencing its fixed read-only **Text** property, like this:

MsgBox Range("A1").Text

Activity

In Excel, only one workbook can be active at any time, only one worksheet can be active at any time, and only one cell can be active at any time. VBA recognizes this, and provides these useful **Application** properties that allow you to write code that is not specific to any particular workbook, worksheet, or range:

Property:	Description:
ActiveWorkbook	The active workbook
ActiveSheet	The active worksheet or chart
ActiveCell	The active cell
ActiveChart	The active chart sheet or chart
ActiveWindow	The active window
Selection	The selected object
ThisWorkbook	The workbook containing this VBA code

You can use the Object Browser in the Visual Basic Editor to discover properties of an object. Select **View**, **Object Browser** or press **F2**.

Try running **MsgBox ActiveSheet.Name** to see the current worksheet name, and **MsgBox ActiveCell.Text** to see the content of the currently selected cell.

Identifying a Range

The VBA **Range( )** method enables you to reference a single cell, or a range of cells, according to what is specified in its **( )** parentheses – a single specified "argument" enclosed between double-quote marks will reference a single cell, but two arguments will identify the start and end of a range of cells.

A single argument to the **Range( )** method can specify a cell by position, such as **"A1"**, or by name – if the cell has been named. A single argument can reference multiple cells by specifying their position as a comma-separated list. A single argument can also reference a cell at the intersection of two specified ranges separated by a space. Additionally, a single argument can specify a range of cells by their start and end position separated by a colon, such as **"A1:C1"**. Two arguments to the **Range( )** method can identify a range of cells by their start and end position separated by a comma, such as **"A1","C1"**.

The **Range( )** method can be dot-suffixed to a specific worksheet object, such as **Worksheets("Sheet1")**, or to the active worksheet object **ActiveSheet**, but these can optionally be omitted as Excel will assume the VBA code is referencing the active worksheet.

Each cell has a **Clear** property that can be used to remove content and styles, and an **Interior.Color** property that can be assigned a Visual Basic constant value to set its background color:

Hot tip

In programming terms, a function or method that can accept different numbers of arguments is termed as "overloaded".

SetRange.xlsm

Don't forget

You can use the Object Browser in the Visual Basic Editor to discover methods of an object. Select **View**, **Object Browser** or press **F2**.

1 Start a new blank worksheet, then open the **Visual Basic Editor** and add a module to the project

2 Select **Module1** in Project Explorer, then type this code in the Code Window to create a macro named "SetRange"
Sub SetRange ( )

' Statements to be inserted here (Steps 3-10).

End Sub

3 Insert a statement to remove content and styles
Worksheets("Sheet1").Range("A1:C8").Clear

4 Insert a statement to reference a single cell by its position
Worksheets("Sheet1").Range("A1").Interior.Color = vbRed

...cont'd

5 Next, insert a statement to name a single cell
`ActiveSheet.Range( "B1" ).Name = "TopCell"`

6 Now, insert a statement to reference a cell by its name
`ActiveSheet.Range( "TopCell" ).Interior.Color = vbGreen`

7 Insert a statement to reference a cell at an intersection
`ActiveSheet.Range( "A1:C1 C1:C3" ).Interior.Color = vbBlue`

8 Then, insert a statement to reference multiple cells by their position – omitting the worksheet object
`Range( "B3,A4,C4" ).Interior.Color = vbYellow`

9 Insert a statements to reference a range of cells, by specifying the range as a single argument
`Range( "A6:C6" ).Interior.Color = vbMagenta`

10 Finally, insert a statement to reference a range of cells, by specifying its start and end as two arguments
`Range( "A8" , "C8" ).Interior.Color = vbCyan`

11 Run the macro to see the individual cells and cell ranges identified, and background colors applied to them

If the active sheet is not a worksheet, statements that call upon the **Range( )** method will produce an error.

You can specify a range as either one or two arguments and the result will be the same.

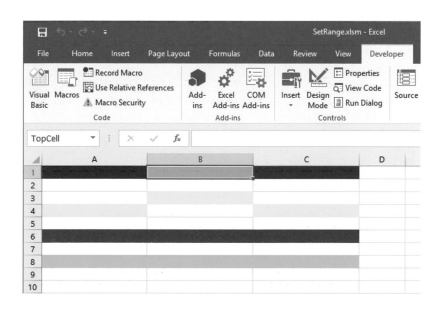

Addressing Cells

The VBA worksheet's **Cells** object represents all cells on the worksheet. It has a **Clear** property that can be used to remove content and styles, and a **HorizontalAlignment** property that can be assigned an Excel constant value to set cell content alignment.

The **Cells( )** method enables you to reference a single cell, according to what is specified in its **( )** parentheses. A single specified argument will reference a single cell by its sequential position in the worksheet within the range of 1-17,179,869,184. More usefully, two arguments will reference a single cell by its row number and numerical or alphabetical column position.

The **Cells( )** method can also be used to specify arguments to the **Range( )** method. For example, instead of specifying a range of cells with **Range("A1" , "C1")** you can specify the same range with **Range(Cells(1, "A") , Cells(1, "C"))**.

A **Select** property can be dot-suffixed to the **Cells( )** method to select an identified cell. The **Cells( )** method can then be used to reference cells sequential to the selected active cell. Alternatively, an **Offset( )** method can be used to reference a cell relative to the selected active cell by specifying row and column argument values:

Hot tip

The maximum size of an Excel worksheet is 1,048,576 rows and 16,384 columns – a total of 17,179,869,184 cells!

SetCells.xlsm

1 Start a new blank worksheet, then open the **Visual Basic Editor** and add a module to the project

2 Select **Module1** in Project Explorer, then type this code in the Code Window to create a macro named "SetCells"
Sub SetCells ( )

' Statements to be inserted here (Steps 3-11).

End Sub

3 Insert a statement to remove content and styles
Worksheets("Sheet1").Cells.Clear

4 Insert a statement to center all cell content
Worksheets("Sheet1").Cells.HorizontalAlignment = xlCenter

5 Next, insert a statement to reference the very first cell on the worksheet by its sequential number
ActiveSheet.Cells(1).Interior.Color = vbMagenta

6 Now, insert a statement to reference a cell by its position
`ActiveSheet.Cells( 2 , 2 ).Interior.Color = vbCyan`

7 Then, insert a statement to reference another cell by its position – omitting the worksheet object
`Cells( 3 , "C" ).Interior.Color = vbYellow`

The **Cells( )** method is especially useful for referencing cells in loop constructs, which are introduced in Chapter Five.

8 Insert statements to reference sequential cells in a range
`Range( Cells( 2 , "D" ) , Cells( 2 , "F" ) ).Cells( 1 ) = "A"`
`Range( Cells( 2 , "D" ) , Cells( 2 , "F" ) ).Cells( 2 ) = "B"`
`Range( Cells( 2 , "D" ) , Cells( 2 , "F" ) ).Cells( 3 ) = "C"`

9 Next, insert a statement to select an identified cell
`Cells( 1 , 7 ).Select`

10 Now, insert statements to reference cells sequential to the selected active cell
`ActiveCell.Cells( 1 ).Interior.Color = vbRed`
`ActiveCell.Cells( 2 ).Interior.Color = vbGreen`
`ActiveCell.Cells( 3 ).Interior.Color = vbBlue`

11 Finally, insert statements to reference cells relative to the selected active cell
`ActiveCell.Offset( 0 , 1 ).Value = 1`
`ActiveCell.Offset( 1 , 1 ).Value = 2`
`ActiveCell.Offset( 2 , 1 ).Value = 3`

Notice that each cell has a **Value** property that can be used to assign values and read values. Each cell also has a read-only **Text** property.

12 Run the macro to see the individual cells identified, and background colors or content applied to them

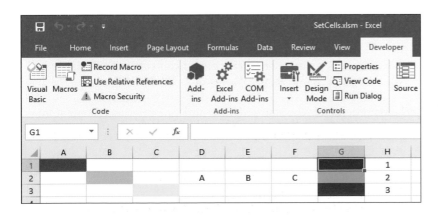

Summary

- The Visual Basic Editor provides a **Project Explorer** that displays a tree view of contents within a selected project.

- Macro VBA code can be written in a module within the Visual Basic Editor's **Code Window**.

- A single VBA module can contain multiple declarations, subroutines, and functions.

- A subroutine code block begins with the keyword **Sub** followed by a programmer-specified name and **( )** parentheses.

- The built-in **MsgBox** function enables you to display a message in a label on a dialog box containing an appropriate icon.

- A macro can be assigned to a button on Excel's **Quick Access Toolbar** for convenience.

- **Form Controls** are graphical interface components that can be added to a worksheet for interaction with the user.

- A macro can be assigned to a **Button** control on a worksheet.

- Everything in Excel is an object within a hierarchical relationship that has an **Application** top-level object.

- Inside the **Application** level is a workbook object that can be referenced by **Workbooks( )**, **ThisWorkbook**, or **ActiveWorkbook**.

- Inside the workbook object is a worksheet object that can be referenced by **WorkSheets( )**, **Sheets( )**, or **ActiveSheet**.

- Cell object properties include **Name**, **Value**, and **Text**.

- The **Range( )** and **Cells( )** methods have a **Select** property that can select a cell, and **ActiveCell** can reference the selected cell.

- Arguments to the **Range( )** method can reference a single cell by position, name, or intersection.

- Arguments to the **Range( )** method can reference a range of cells or multiple cells in a comma-separated list.

- The **Cells** object represents all cells on a worksheet.

- Arguments to the **Cells( )** method can reference a single cell by its worksheet position or by its sequential position.

3 Storing values

This chapter demonstrates how to store various types of data within VBA macros.

Creating variables

A variable is a container in a VBA macro in which a data value can be stored inside the computer's memory. The stored value can be referenced using the variable's identifier name, and new values can be assigned as the macro runs. The programmer can choose any name for a variable providing it adheres to the naming conventions listed in the table below:

Naming rule:	Example:
CANNOT contain any of the keywords	**Next**
CANNOT contain arithmetic operators	**a+b*c**
CANNOT contain punctuation characters	**%$#@!**
CANNOT contain any spaces	**no spaces**
CANNOT start with a number	**2bad**
CAN contain numbers elsewhere	**good1**
CAN contain mixed case	**UPdown**
CAN contain underscores	**is_ok**

Hot tip

Variable names can be up to 254 characters in length, but shorter names are recommended.

Beware

VBA is not case-sensitive so you should avoid using variable names that differ only by case.

It is good practice to choose meaningful names for variables to make the VBA macro code more easily understood. Lengthy variable names may comprise several words, and can be made more readable by using a "CamelCase" naming convention. This joins together multiple words to form a variable name in which the first letter of every word is capitalized, e.g. **MyFirstVariable**. Alternatively, you may prefer to use all lowercase and separate the words with an underscore character, e.g. **my_first_variable**. Choose the variable naming convention you prefer and use it consistently in all your VBA macro code.

A variable is created by simply assigning a value to a valid name in a variable "declaration", like this:

```
OneDozen = 12
IsValid = True
user_name = "Mike McGrath"
```

The table below lists 60 keywords that have special significance in VBA programming – they cannot be used as identifier names in macro code:

Keywords:			
And	As	Base	Boolean
Byte	ByVal	Call	Case
Const	Date	Debug	Dim
Do	Double	Each	Else
ElseIf	End	Error	Exit
Explicit	False	For	Function
GoTo	If	In	Integer
Is	Long	Loop	Me
Mod	Next	Not	Nothing
Object	On	Option	Optional
Or	ParamArray	Preserve	Print
Private	Public	ReDim	Resume
Select	Set	Static	String
Sub	Then	To	True
Until	While	With	Xor

Hot tip

To find a list of all keywords, click **Help** in the Visual Basic Editor and open the online help web page, then search for "VBA keywords".

There are, in fact, many more keywords in the Visual Basic language, but the 60 listed above are the common keywords that are used by the examples in this book.

Defining data types

Variables can store different types of data, such as integer whole numbers, floating-point numbers, strings of text, and Boolean values of true or false. When data is assigned to a valid variable name in a declaration, VBA will, by default, automatically create a variable of the type appropriate for the assigned data. Each data type is allocated a number of bytes in memory for data storage. The table below lists the common VBA data types, together with the size of their allocated memory and possible range of values:

Use the **Long** data type for Excel row numbers, as they exceed the maximum range of the **Integer** data type.

Data Type:	Size:	Range:
Byte	1 byte	0 to 255
Boolean	2 bytes	**True** or **False**
Integer	2 bytes	-32,768 to 32,767
Long	4 bytes	-2,147,483,648 to 2,147,483,647
Double	8 bytes	-1.79769313486231570E+308 to -4.94065645841246544E-324 and 4.94065645841246544E-324 to 1.79769313486231570E+308
Date	8 bytes	0:00:00 January 1, 0001 to 11:59:59 December 31, 9999
String	string length	0 to 2 billion Unicode characters

When a variable is assigned an initial value, it is said to have been "initialized". A variable declaration that defines a data type cannot be assigned a value in the declaration – it must be initialized in a separate statement.

Optionally, a variable declaration can specify the data type that variable may contain. This reserves the appropriate memory space before a value is assigned to the variable in a subsequent statement. The declaration requires the **Dim** (dimension) keyword before the variable name, and **As** keyword before the data type:

Dim *variable-name* **As** *data-type*

For example:
Dim OneDozen As Integer
Dim IsValid As Boolean
Dim user_name As String

...cont'd

If a variable declaration does not specify a data type, the variable is created as a **Variant** type to which any kind of data can be assigned. Unless a **Variant** type is specifically required, this can allocate unnecessary memory space and so be inefficient.

To enforce good practice it is recommended you always add this directive at the very start of the module, before any other code:
Option Explicit

The VBA compiler then generates an error if you attempt to create a variable that does not have a defined data type.

You can reference the value contained in a variable using its name, and discover the data type of any variable by supplying its name as an argument to the built-in **TypeName( )** function:

43

1 Begin a VBA macro module by enforcing data types
Option Explicit

2 Then, add a subroutine that declares a variable
Sub FirstVar( )

    Dim OneDozen As Integer
    ' Statements to be inserted here (Steps 3 & 4).

    End Sub

3 Next, insert a statement to assign an initial value
OneDozen = 12

4 Now, insert statements to reference the stored value and to discover the variable's data type
MsgBox OneDozen , vbOKOnly , "Value"
MsgBox TypeName(OneDozen) , vbOKOnly , "Data Type"

5 Finally, run the macro to see the variable's value and data type

Always use **Option Explicit** as it also prevents errors of mis-spelled variable names.

FirstVar.xlsm

You can have the Visual Basic Editor automatically add **Option Explicit** at the start of every module by checking the **Require Variable Declaration** option on the **Editor** tab under **Tools**, **Options**.

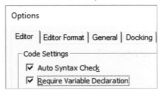

Managing strings

Text assigned to a **String** variable must always be enclosed within " " double quote marks, to denote the start and end of the string. Strings can be concatenated (joined) together simply by using the **&** concatenation operator to form a new longer string.

VBA has several built-in functions that can be used to manage strings. You can find the length of a string by specifying the **String** variable's name as an argument to the built-in **Len( )** function, and surrounding whitespace can be removed by the **Trim( )** function. This is useful when dealing with user input which may have surrounding space characters accidentally included. The case of any string can be changed to lowercase by the **LCase( )** function, or to uppercase by the **UCase( )** function. This is useful when making comparisons, to ensure matching text. You can search a string to seek a substring by specifying the **String** variable's name, and the substring, as arguments to the **InStr( )** function.

Dates in VBA have their own **Date** data type, and values must be assigned in month/day/year format enclosed within **# #** hash characters. Usefully, parts of a **Date** value can be assigned to a String variable by specifying the **Date** variable's name and a format specifier as arguments to the built-in **Format( )** function:

Date & Time Format Specifiers:		Example:
m	Month number	2
mmmm	Month name	February
d	Day number	14
dddd	Day name	Tuesday
yyyy	Full year	2018
hh	Hour, with zeros	08
nn	Minute, with zeros	05
ss	Second, with zeros	03
am/pm	Current meridiem	am

1 Begin a VBA macro module with a subroutine that declares a string variable

Sub StringDate( )

Dim Str As String
' **Statements to be inserted here (Steps 2-6).**

End Sub

StringDate.xlsm

2 Next, insert statements to initialize the variable, concatenate strings, and remove surrounding whitespace

Str = " Database "
Str = " Excel " & Str
Str = Trim(Str)

3 Now, insert statements to display the new trimmed string value and its total number of characters

Range("A1").Value = Str
Range("B1").Value = Len(Str)

4 Insert statements to change the string case and seek two substrings, then display the new string and search results

Str = LCase(Str)
Range("A2").Value = Str
Range("B2").Value = InStr(Str , "data")
Range("C2").Value = InStr(Str , "Data")

The second search will fail because the string has been converted to lowercase.

5 Next, declare and initialize a date variable

Dim Valentine As Date
Valentine = #2/14/2018#

6 Now, display the date, and a formatted part of the date

Range("A3").Value = Valentine
Str = Format(Valentine , "mmmm, d")
Range("B3").Value = Str

Notice that the result of the search returns the index position of the first character within the string at which the substring is found, or zero if the substring is not found.

7 Finally, run the macro to see the strings and dates

◢	A	B	C	D
1	Excel Database	18		
2	excel database	11	0	
3	2/14/2018	February, 14		

45

Producing arrays

An array variable can store multiple items of data, unlike a regular variable that can only store a single item of data.

The items of data are stored sequentially in array "elements" that are, by default, numbered starting at zero. So, the first array value is stored in array element zero, the second array value is stored in array element one, and so on.

An array variable is declared in a VBA macro in the same way as regular variables, but additionally, the index number of the final element can be specified in the declaration to establish the array size. This is stated as an argument within parentheses following the array name, with this syntax:

Dim *array-name* (*final-index*) **As** *data-type*

Each element of a declared array can then be assigned a value by stating the array name and index number within parentheses:

array-name (*index*) = *value*

It is often desirable to create an array whose elements are numbered starting at an index number other than zero. This is simply achieved by stating the index number of the first and final elements as a declaration argument using the **To** keyword:

Dim *array-name*(*first-index* **To** *final-index*) **As** *data-type*

If you would prefer to have VBA always start array index numbering at one, rather than zero, you can add this directive at the very start of the module, before any other code:

Option Base 1

Optionally, an array declaration may omit an argument from its parentheses to create a "dynamic" array. The size of that array can be established later using the **ReDim** keyword before its elements are assigned values. The array can be resized repeatedly using the **ReDim** keyword, but its element values will be lost unless the statement includes the **Preserve** keyword:

Dim *array-name* ( ) **As** *data-type*

ReDim *array-name*(*first-index* **To** *final-index*)

ReDim Preserve *array-name*(*first-index* **To** *final-index*)

If your code attempts to reference an element index number that does not exist, VBA will present a "Subscript out of range" error dialog box when you try to run the macro.

Microsoft Visual Basic

Run-time error '9':

Subscript out of range

Continue   End   Debug   Help

The true advantage of array variables is demonstrated later with loop constructs – introduced in Chapter Five.

...cont'd

1 Begin a VBA macro module with a subroutine that declares a string array of three elements

```
Sub FirstArray( )

Dim Fruit( 2 ) As String
' Statements to be inserted here (Steps 2-6).

End Sub
```

FirstArray.xlsm

2 Next, insert statements to initialize each array element and display the value in the element at index number one

```
Fruit( 0 ) = "Apple"
Fruit( 1 ) = "Banana"
Fruit( 2 ) = "Cherry"
Range( "A1" ).Text = "First Fruit: " & Fruit( 1 )
```

The **Text** property of a cell is what it displays but is not necessarily the same as its **Value** property, which is stored internally and used for formulas and calculations.

3 Now, declare another string array of three elements, this time specifying its first and final index numbers

```
Dim Veg( 1 To 3 ) As String
```

4 Insert statements to initialize each array element and display the value in the element at index number one

```
Veg( 1 ) = "Artichoke"
Veg( 2 ) = "Broccoli"
Veg( 3 ) = "Cabbage"
Range( "B1" ).Text = "First Veg: " & Veg( 1 )
```

5 Next, declare a dynamic string array, then establish its size by specifying its first and final index numbers

```
Dim Flower( ) As String
ReDim Flower( 1 To 3 )
```

6 Now, insert statements to initialize each array element and display the value in the element at the final index number

```
Flower( 1 ) = "Azalea"
Flower( 2 ) = "Buttercup"
Flower( 3 ) = "Crocus"
Range( "C1" ).Text = "Final Flower: " & Flower( 3 )
```

The first element in the **Fruit** array is index number zero, so index number one references that array's <u>second</u> element.

7 Finally, run the macro to see the array element values

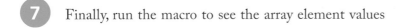

	A	B	C	D
1	First Fruit: Banana	First Veg: Artichoke	Final Flower: Crocus	
2				

47

Describing dimensions

An array created with a single index is a one-dimensional array in which the elements appear in a single row:

Element content...	A	B	C	D	E
Index numbers...	(0)	(1)	(2)	(3)	(4)

Arrays can also have multiple indices – to represent multiple dimensions. An array created with two indices is a two-dimensional array in which the elements appear in multiple rows:

First index	(0)	A	B	C	D	E
	(1)	F	G	H	I	J
Second index		(0)	(1)	(2)	(3)	(4)

With multi-dimensional arrays, the value contained in each element is referenced by stating the number of each index. For example, with the two-dimensional array above, the element at **(1, 2)** contains the letter H.

Two-dimensional arrays are useful in Excel VBA to store row and column information, in which the first index represents rows and the second index represents columns.

Multi-dimensional arrays are created in the same way as one-dimensional arrays, except they must specify the size of each index as comma-separated arguments in the declaration, like this:

Dim *array-name* (*final* , *final* , *final*) **As** *data-type*

It is often useful to create each index with elements numbered starting at an index number other than zero. This can be achieved by stating the index number of the first and final elements of each index in the declaration argument, using the **To** keyword:

Dim *array-name* (*first* **To** *final* , *first* **To** *final*) **As** *data-type*

Alternatively, you can have VBA always start each array index numbering at one, rather than zero, by adding this directive at the very start of the module, before any other code:

Option Base 1

Multi-dimensional arrays of up to 60 indices are possible, but arrays of more than three indices are uncommon.

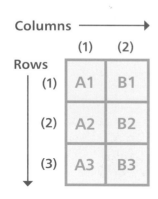

Arrays of more than three indices are difficult to envision.

1 Begin a VBA macro module by adding an initial directive to start index numbering at one
Option Base 1

Array2D.xlsm

2 Next, add a subroutine that declares a two-dimensional string array of three elements in each index
Sub Array2D( )

Dim Basket(3 , 3) As String
' Statements to be inserted here (Steps 3-6).

End Sub

Hot tip

As with one-dimensional arrays, you can also first declare a dynamic array. The size of each index can then be established in a **ReDim** statement.

3 Now, insert statements to initialize each array element in the first index
Basket(1 , 1) = "Apple"
Basket(1 , 2) = "Banana"
Basket(1 , 3) = "Cherry"

4 Then, insert statements to initialize each array element in the second index
Basket(2 , 1) = "Artichoke"
Basket(2 , 2) = "Broccoli"
Basket(2 , 3) = "Cabbage"

5 Insert statements to display the first index values on the first row of a worksheet
Range("A1").Value = Basket(1 , 1)
Range("B1").Value = Basket(1 , 2)
Range("C1").Value = Basket(1 , 3)

Don't forget

The assignment of individual array elements to individual cells may seem tedious, and indeed it is – later examples demonstrate how to assign multiple elements to multiple cells much more efficiently.

6 Finally, insert statements to display the second index values on the second row of a worksheet
Range("A2").Value = Basket(2 , 1)
Range("B2").Value = Basket(2 , 2)
Range("C2").Value = Basket(2 , 3)

7 Run the macro to see the array element values

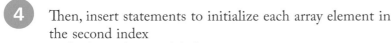

	A	B	C	D
1	Apple	Banana	Cherry	
2	Artichoke	Broccoli	Cabbage	
3				

49

Representing objects

In addition to regular variables and array variables, VBA provides a special "object variable". These can represent an entire Excel object, such as a **Worksheet** or a **Range**. An object variable declaration is similar to a regular variable declaration, except it specifies an object type, rather than a data type, with this syntax:

Dim *variable-name* **As** *object-type*

Assignments of the appropriate object type can then be made to the object variable using the **Set** keyword, like this:

Set *variable-name* = *object*

Object variables of the **Range** object type are most useful for transferring data from worksheet cells to VBA variables, and back again. For this purpose, a **Range** object has a **Resize( )** method that can be used to accommodate a number of rows and columns specified as its two arguments.

A variable of the (default) **Variant** type can first be assigned row and column values by the **Range( )** method – copying data from worksheet cells into a variable. It is important to recognize that this will always create a two-dimensional array, in which the first index represents the rows and the second index represents the columns. This is true even when the assignment is of only a single row, or a single column, or even just a single cell.

The array into which the worksheet data is assigned will always have the ability to contain one value in each index. This is known as the array index's "lower boundary". It can be referenced using the **LBound( )** method to specify the array name and index number as its two arguments. More usefully, its companion **UBound( )** method can specify the array name and index number as its two arguments to reference the "upper boundary" of an array index – to establish the number of elements in that array index.

Having the ability to establish the size of an array index means that the **UBound( )** method can be used as an argument to a **Range** object's **Resize( )** method to match the size of the array and the size of the **Range** object. The entire array can then be assigned to the like-sized **Range** object – copying data from a VBA variable back into worksheet cells.

A variable of the **Variant** type can be assigned any kind of data, but this type should only be used where specifically required.

The **LBound( )** and **UBound( )** methods return the "dimensions" of an array index.

...cont'd

1 First, fill worksheet cells A1:C5 with values

◢	A	B	C	D	E	F	G	H	I	J
1	101	201	301							
2	102	202	302							
3	103	203	303							
4	104	204	304							
5	105	205	305							

ObjectVar.xlsm

2 Begin a VBA module with a subroutine that declares an object variable and an array variable

```
Sub ObjectVar( )

Dim Obj As Range
Dim Data As Variant
' Statements to be inserted here (Steps 3-5).

End Sub
```

3 Next, insert statements to read and write a single column

```
Data = Range( "A1:A5" )
Set Obj = Range( "E1" )
Set Obj = Obj.Resize( UBound( Data , 1 ) , 1 )
Obj.Value = Data
```

4 Now, insert statements to read and write a single row

```
Data = Range( "A1:C1" )
Set Obj = Range( "G1" )
Set Obj = Obj.Resize( 1, UBound( Data , 2 ) )
Obj.Value = Data
```

5 Finally, insert statements to read and write multiple rows and columns

```
Data = Range( "A1:C3" )
Set Obj = Range( "G3" )
Set Obj = Obj.Resize( UBound( Data, 1) , UBound( Data, 2) )
Obj.Value = Data
```

6 Run the macro to see the transferred values

◢	A	B	C	D	E	F	G	H	I	J
1	101	201	301		101		101	201	301	
2	102	202	302		102					
3	103	203	303		103		101	201	301	
4	104	204	304		104		102	202	302	
5	105	205	305		105		103	203	303	

Hot tip

The **Range** object is resized in Step 3 to hold 5 rows and 1 column.

The **Range** object is resized in Step 4 to hold 1 row and 3 columns.

The **Range** object is resized in Step 5 to hold 3 rows and 3 columns.

Declaring constants

The value stored within a variable container may change for other values of the same data type as the VBA macro executes its code. Where the macro uses a value that will not change during its execution, it is good programming practice to store that value inside a "constant" container, rather than inside a variable.

A constant is declared using the **Const** keyword, followed by a programmer-specified name and a VBA data type. Unlike variable declarations, a constant declaration should also assign a value:

Const *constant-name* **As** *data-type* = *value*

Constants can make your code more readable, by using the constant name in statements, and make code easier to maintain. For example, if the code refers to a fixed tax rate, its value is best stored in a constant whose name can be used throughout the code. Should the tax rate ever change, the code can be updated simply by assigning the new rate to the constant:

1 Begin a VBA macro module with a subroutine that declares a constant for a tax rate of 7%, plus two variables
Sub FirstConst( )

Const TaxRate As Double = 0.07
Dim Price As Double
Dim Tax As Double
' **Statements to be inserted here (Steps 2 & 3).**

End Sub

2 Next, insert statements to initialize each variable
Price = ActiveCell.Value
Tax = Price * TaxRate

3 Now, insert statements to display the tax and total
ActiveCell.Offset(1 , 0) = Tax
ActiveCell.Offset(2 , 0) = Price + Tax

4 Select a cell containing a currency value, then run the macro to see the calculated tax and total

	A	B	C
1	50.00		
2	3.50		
3	53.50		

A1

VBA provides lots of predefined constants that you can freely use in your code. These constant names each have a "vb" prefix – for example, the **vbRed** color constant seen on page 15. Excel provides additional constants that you can also use in your macros, and these each have an "xl" prefix – for example, **xlCenter**. You can explore or search for VBA and Excel constants using the Object Browser in the Visual Basic Editor:

1 Open the Visual Basic Editor, then select **View, Object Browser** on the menu bar, or press **F2** – to open the Object Browser window

2 In the top drop-down box, select **VBA** or **Excel** to choose the Library you wish to search, or choose **<All Libraries>**

3 Next, type "constants" in the bottom drop-down box, then hit the 🔍 search button

4 When the search results appear, select the **Class** you wish to search to see its predefined constant Members listed

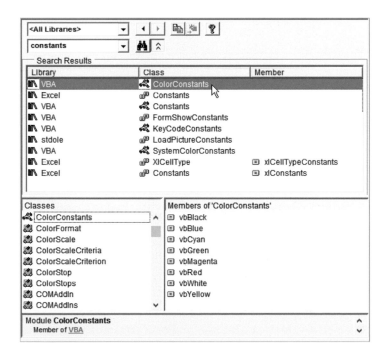

The macro recorder writes code that includes predefined VBA and Excel constants, so it's useful to examine recorded macro code to discover which constants are used for any particular purpose.

IntelliSense also provides some pop-up constant suggestions when you are writing code. Ensure you have **Auto List Members** enabled in **Tools**, **Options**, **Editor**.

Summary

- A variable is a named container in which data can be stored, and the data can be referenced using the variable's name.

- When naming variables, the programmer should choose a meaningful name that adheres to the naming conventions.

- A variable declaration can specify the type of data that may be stored in that variable, such as **Integer**, **Double**, or **Boolean**.

- If a variable declaration does not specify a data type, a **Variant** type variable is created, which can store any kind of data.

- Starting macro code with an **Option Explicit** directive ensures that variable declarations must specify a data type.

- Values assigned to a **String** variable must be enclosed within " " double quote marks to denote the start and end of text.

- Values assigned to a **Date** variable must be enclosed within # # hash marks and be in month/day/year format.

- An array can store multiple values in individual elements that can be referenced using the array name and index number.

- Array index numbering begins at zero by default, but adding an **Option Base 1** directive begins index numbering at one.

- An array variable declaration should specify the size of its index by stating the number of elements as its argument.

- Multi-dimensional array declarations should specify the size of each index as comma-separated arguments.

- Two-dimensional arrays are useful to store row information in the first index and column information in the second index.

- An object variable can represent an entire **Worksheet** or **Range** and requires the **Set** keyword when making assignments.

- The **Range( )** method can be used to assign cell values to a variable of the **Variant** data type.

- A **Range** object can be resized to match the upper boundary of an array index using the **UBound( )** method.

- Fixed values can be assigned to a constant variable in a declaration using the **Const** keyword.

4 Performing operations

This chapter introduces VBA operators, and demonstrates the operations they can perform.

Doing arithmetic

The arithmetical operators used in VBA are listed in the table below, together with a description of the arithmetic they perform:

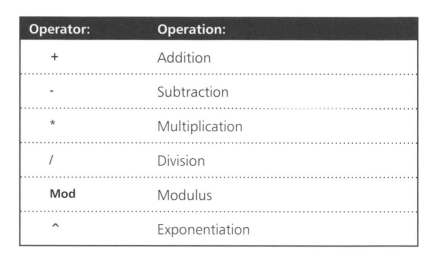

Operator:	Operation:
+	Addition
-	Subtraction
*	Multiplication
/	Division
Mod	Modulus
^	Exponentiation

The operators for addition, subtraction, multiplication and division act as you would expect. Care must be taken, however, to group expressions where more than one operator is used to clarify the expression. For example, with this expression:

result = 4 + 8 * 2 - 6 / 3

The desired order in which the operations should be performed is unclear, but if performed by default order it produces:

4 + 16 - 2 = 18

The desired order can be clarified by adding parentheses, like this:

result = ((4 + 8) * 2) - (6 / 3)

Operations within innermost parentheses are performed first, so the expression now produces:

(12 * 2) - (6 / 3)
24 - 2 = 22

The **Mod** modulus operator will divide the first operand by the second operand and return the remainder of the operation. This is useful to determine if a number has an odd or even value. The ^ exponentiation operator returns the result of the first operand raised to the power of the second operand.

The **+** operator is dual purpose, as it performs addition on numbers and concatenation on strings.

Values used with operators to form expressions are called "operands" – in the expression **2 + 3** the numerical values **2** and **3** are the operands.

1 Begin a VBA macro module with a subroutine that
declares and initializes two variables

```
Sub Arithmetic( )

    Dim a As Integer
    Dim b As Integer
    a = 8
    b = 4

    ' Statements to be inserted here (Steps 2-5).

End Sub
```

Arithmetic.xlsm

2 Next, insert statements to display the result of addition
and subtraction

```
Range( "A1:C1" ) = _
        Array( "Addition:" , "8 + 4 =" , ( a + b ) )
Range( "A2:C2" ) = _
        Array( "Subtraction:" , "8 - 4 =" , ( a - b ) )
```

Notice here how the _
underscore character
enables line continuation
of the code.

3 Now, insert statements to display the result of
multiplication and division

```
Range( "A3:C3" ) = _
        Array( "Multiplication:" , "8 * 4 =" , ( a * b ) )
Range( "A4:C4" ) = _
        Array( "Division:" , "8 / 4 =" , ( a / b ) )
```

4 Then, insert a statement to display a modulus result

```
Range( "A5:C5" ) = _
        Array( "Modulus:" , "8 Mod 4 =" , ( a Mod b ) )
```

The **Array( )** method is
used here to create each
array of three elements,
which matches each
range of three cells.

5 Finally, insert a statement to display an exponent result

```
Range( "A6:C6" ) = _
        Array( "Exponent:" , "8 ^ 4 =" , ( a ^ b ) )
```

6 Run the macro to see the result of arithmetic operations

	A	B	C
1	Addition:	8 + 4 = 12	
2	Subtraction:	8 - 4 = 4	
3	Multiplication:	8 * 4 = 32	
4	Division:	8 / 4 = 2	
5	Modulus:	8 Mod 4 = 0	
6	Exponent:	8 ^ 4 = 4096	

Making comparisons

The comparison operators used in VBA are listed in the table below, together with a description of the comparison they make:

Operator:	Operation:
=	Equal To (Equality)
<>	Not Equal To (Inequality)
>	Greater Than
<	Less Than
>=	Greater Than Or Equal To
<=	Less Than Or Equal To

Each comparison operator returns a Boolean value of **True** or **False** according to the result of the comparison made. The = Equality operator compares two operands and will return **True** if both are equal in value, otherwise it will return a **False** value. If both are the same number, they are equal, or if both are strings, the ASCII code values of their characters are compared numerically to achieve the comparison result.

Conversely, the <> Inequality operator returns **True** if two operands are not equal, using the same rules as the = equality operator, otherwise it returns **False**. Equality and Inequality operators are useful in testing the state of two variables to perform conditional branching in a macro according to the result.

The > Greater Than operator compares two operands and will return **True** if the first is greater in value than the second, or it will return **False** if it is equal or less in value. The < Less Than operator makes the same comparison but returns **True** if the first operand is less in value than the second, otherwise it returns **False**. A > Greater Than or < Less Than operator is often used to test the value of an iteration counter in a loop construct.

Adding the = Equality operator after a > Greater Than or < Less Than operator makes it also return **True** if the two operands are exactly equal in value.

...cont'd

1 Begin a VBA macro module with a subroutine that declares and initializes five variables

```
Sub Comparison( )

    Dim Nil As Integer
    Dim Num As Integer
    Dim Max As Integer
    Dim Lower As String
    Dim Upper As String

    Nil = 0
    Num = 0
    Max = 1
    Lower = "a"
    Upper = "A"

    ' Statements to be inserted here (Steps 2 & 3).

End Sub
```

Comparison.xlsm

2 Next, insert statements to display the result of equality and inequality comparisons

```
Range( "A1:C1" ) = _
        Array( "Equality:" , "0 = 0" , ( Nil = Num ) )
Range( "A2:C2" ) = _
        Array( "Equality:" , "a = A" , ( Lower = Upper ) )
Range( "A3:C3" ) = _
        Array( "Inequality:" , "0 <> 1" , ( Nil <> Max ) )
```

Comparison of strings that contain multiple characters also take character order into account – so that "ABC" is not equal to "BAC".

3 Now, insert statements to display the result of greater and less comparisons

```
Range( "A4:C4" ) = _
        Array( "Greater:" , "0 > 1" , ( Nil > Max ) )
Range( "A5:C5" ) = _
        Array( "Less:" , "0 < 1" , ( Nil < Max ) )
Range( "A6:C6" ) = _
        Array( "Less Or Equal:" , "0 <= 1" , ( Nil <= Max ) )
```

4 Run the macro to see the result of comparison operations

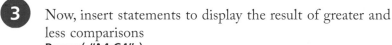

	A	B	C
1	Equality:	0 = 0	TRUE
2	Equality:	a = A	FALSE
3	Inequality:	0 <> 1	TRUE
4	Greater:	0 > 1	FALSE
5	Less:	0 < 1	TRUE
6	Less Or Equal:	0 <= 1	TRUE

Assessing logic

The logical operators used in VBA are listed in the table below, together with a description of the operation they perform:

Operator:	Operation:
And	Logical AND conjunction
Or	Logical OR disjunction
Xor	Logical XOR exclusion
Not	Logical NOT negation

Hot tip

The term "Boolean" refers to a system of logical thought developed by the English mathematician George Boole (1815-1864).

The logical operators are used with operands that have Boolean values of **True** or **False**, or expressions that convert to **True** or **False**.

The (logical AND) **And** operator will evaluate two operands and return **True** only if both operands themselves are **True**. Otherwise, the **And** operator will return **False**. This is useful in conditional branching where the direction of a macro is determined by testing two conditions – if both conditions are satisfied, the macro will go in a certain direction, otherwise it will take a different direction.

Unlike the **And** operator, which needs both operands to be **True**, the (logical OR) **Or** operator will evaluate its two operands and return **True** if either one, or both, of the operands itself returns **True**. If neither operand returns **True**, then the **Or** operator will return **False**. This is useful in VBA to perform a certain action if either one of two test conditions has been met. The (logical XOR) **Xor** operator works in a similar way, but will only return **True** if either one of the operands return **True**, but not if both return **True**.

The (logical NOT) **Not** operator is a unary operator that is used before a single operand. It returns the inverse value of the given operand, so if variable **A** had a value of **True**, then **Not A** would have a value of **False**. The **Not** operator is useful in VBA to toggle the value of a variable in successive loop iterations with a statement like **A = Not A**. This ensures that on each iteration of the loop, the Boolean value is reversed, like flicking a light switch on and off.

1 Begin a VBA macro module with a subroutine that declares and initializes two variables

```
Sub Logic( )

Dim Yes As Boolean
Dim No As Boolean

Yes = True
No = False

' Statements to be inserted here (Steps 2-5).

End Sub
```

Logic.xlsm

2 Next, insert a statement to display the result of conjunction

```
Range( "A1:E1" ) = Array( "AND Logic:" , _
        "True And True =" , ( Yes And Yes ) , _
        "True And False =" , ( Yes And No ) )
```

3 Now, insert a statement to display the result of disjunction

```
Range( "A3:E3" ) = Array( "OR Logic:" , _
        "True Or True =" , ( Yes Or Yes ) , _
        "True Or False =" , ( Yes Or No ) )
```

4 Then, insert a statement to display the result of exclusion

```
Range( "A5:E5" ) = Array( "XOR Logic:" , _
        "True Xor True =" , ( Yes Xor Yes ) , _
        "True Xor False =" , ( Yes Xor No ) )
```

5 Finally, insert a statement to display the result of negation

```
Range( "A7:E7" ) = Array( "NOT Logic:" , _
        "Yes =" , Yes , "Not Yes =" , ( Not Yes ) )
```

Note that the expression **False And False** returns **False**, not **True** – perhaps demonstrating the maxim "two wrongs don't make a right".

6 Run the macro to see the result of logical operations

	A	B	C	D	E
1	AND Logic:	True And True =	TRUE	True And False =	FALSE
2					
3	OR Logic:	True Or True =	TRUE	True Or False =	TRUE
4					
5	XOR Logic:	True Xor True =	FALSE	True Xor False =	TRUE
6					
7	NOT Logic:	Yes =	TRUE	Not Yes =	FALSE

Joining strings

VBA provides two possible operators that can be used to concatenate (join) string values:

Do not use the **+** operator for string concatenation, to avoid unexpected results.

- **&** The concatenation operator always regards its operands as string values, even if they are numerical without surrounding quote marks. It will always produce a concatenated string result, and is recommended for joining strings. For example:
  "1" & "2" returns **"12"**
  "1" & 2 also returns **"12"**

- **+** The addition operator does not always regard its operands as string values if one operand is numerical. It may not always produce a concatenated string result, and is recommended for addition only. For example:
  "1" + "2" returns **"12"**
  but **"1" + 2** returns **3**

Concatenated strings simply combine the characters they contain in the sequence in which they are joined together. You may often want to separate the strings with a space, or some other delimiter. By joining together just a few strings, you can concatenate an intermediate string that contains a delimiter, like this:

Concat = Str1 & " " & Str2
Concat = Str1 & " , " & Str2

Each space character in the strings being joined together is preserved in the concatenated string.

When you want to join together many strings, this technique becomes tedious and can produce code that is hard to read. A better alternative is provided by the VBA **Join( )** method, which accepts an array as its first argument. The strings to be joined can be listed as arguments to the **Array( )** method to accomplish this:

Concat = Join(Array(Str1 , Str2 , Str3 , Str4))

Usefully, the **Join( )** method automatically inserts a single space delimiter in the concatenated returned string, but you can specify an alternative delimiter as its second argument, like this:

Concat = Join(Array(Str1 , Str2 , Str3 , Str4) , " , ")

When you want the concatenated returned string to display the individual joined strings on separate lines, the delimiter can be specified as a line break using the **vbNewLine** constant.

1 Begin a VBA macro module with a subroutine that declares five variables

```
Sub JoinStr( )

Dim Name As String
Dim Address As String
Dim City As String
Dim Zip As String
Dim Concat As String

' Statements to be inserted here (Steps 2-5).

End Sub
```

2 Next, insert statements to initialize four variables

```
Name = "Ripley's"
Address = "175 Jefferson St."
City = "San Francisco"
Zip = "CA 94133"
```

3 Now, insert statements to display a concatenated string that separates two variable values by an ellipsis and spaces

```
Concat = Name & " ... " & City
Range( "A1" ) = Concat
```

4 Then, insert statements to display a concatenated string that separates four variable values by a comma and space

```
Concat = Join( Array( Name , Address , City , Zip ) , ", " )
Range( "B1" ) = Concat
```

5 Finally, insert statements to display a concatenated string that separates four variable values by a line break

```
Concat = _
    Join( Array( Name , Address , City , Zip ) , vbNewLine )
Range( "C1" ) = Concat
```

6 Run the macro to see the concatenated strings

	A	B	C
1	Ripley's ... San Francisco	Ripley's, 175 Jefferson St., San Francisco, CA 94133	Ripley's 175 Jefferson St. San Francisco CA 94133
2			

JoinStr.xlsm

Hot tip

You may also see the **vbCrLf** constant used to create line breaks. This does exactly the same as the **vbNewLine** constant. It refers to "CarriageReturn" and "LineFeed" from the days before computers had monitors and all output was printed on paper.

63

To begin a new line, the print carriage had to return to the left edge of the paper, then the paper was fed upwards by one line height. (Illustrated computer is a Philips P320 from 1972.)

Understanding precedence

When an expression contains multiple operators the order in which the individual operations are performed is determined by VBA's default "operator precedence". For example, in the expression **3 * 8 + 4** the default operator precedence determines that multiplication is completed first, so the result is 28 (24 + 4).

The table below lists operator precedence in descending order – those on the top row have highest precedence, those on lower rows have successively lower precedence. Operations are performed for operators with equal precedence (on the same row of the table) from left to right – in the order in which they appear in the expression.

It is good practice to use **( )** parentheses to clarify expressions, rather than rely upon the default order of operator precedence.

Parentheses will also override left to right default order for operators of equal precedence.

Operator:	Operation:	Order:
^	Exponentiation	1
* /	Multiplication Division	2
Mod	Modulus	3
+ -	Addition Subtraction	4
&	Concatenation	5
= <> > < >= <=	Equality Inequality Greater Than Less Than Greater Than Or Equal Less Than Or Equal	6
Not **And** **Or** **Xor**	Logical NOT negation Logical AND conjunction Logical OR disjunction Logical XOR exclusion	7

Expressions that contain parentheses will override the default order of precedence by forcing operations to be performed on the innermost parentheses first, then outer parentheses, then operators outside of parentheses.

...cont'd

1 Begin a VBA macro module with a subroutine that declares and initializes three variables

Sub Precedence( )

Dim A As Integer
Dim B As Integer
Dim C As Integer

A = 8
B = 4
C = 2

' Statements to be inserted here (Steps 2-5).

End Sub

Precedence.xlsm

2 Next, insert a statement to display the result of evaluating an expression using default operator precedence

Range("A1:C1") = Array("Default Order:" , _
    "8 * 4 + 2 =" , (A * B + C))

Notice that the entire expression is enclosed within parentheses for clarity when specifying it as an argument. This does not affect operation order, but simply makes the code more readable.

3 Now, insert a statement to display the result of evaluating a similar expression, but with forced operation order

Range("A2:C2") = Array("Forced Order:" , _
    "8 * (4 + 2) =" , (A * (B + C)))

4 Then, insert a second statement to display the result of evaluating an expression using default operator precedence

Range("A4:C4") = Array("Default Order:" , _
    "8 ^ 4 / 2 =" , (A ^ B / C))

5 Finally, insert a statement to display the result of evaluating another similar expression, but with forced operation order

Range("A5:C5") = Array("Forced Order:" , _
    "8 ^ (4 / 2) =" , (A ^ (B / C)))

6 Run the macro to see the markedly different results

With these results:
32 + 2 = 34
8 * 6 = 48
...and...
4096 / 2 = 2048
8 ^ 2 = 64.

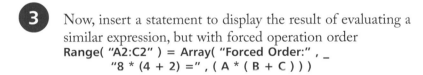

▲	A	B	C	D
1	Default Order:	8 * 4 + 2 = 34		
2	Forced Order:	8 * (4 + 2) = 48		
3				
4	Default Order:	8 ^ 4 / 2 = 2048		
5	Forced Order:	8 ^ (4 / 2) = 64		
6				

Summary

- Arithmetical operators for + addition, - subtraction, * multiplication and / division, all act as expected.

- Expressions grouped within ( ) parentheses for clarity ensure those within innermost parentheses will be evaluated first.

- The **Mod** modulus operator divides the first operand by the second operand, then returns the remainder.

- The ^ exponentiation operator returns the result of the first operand raised to the power of the second operand.

- Comparisons operators for = Equality, <> Inequality, > Greater Than or < Less Than, each return **True** or **False**.

- Adding the = Equality operator after a > Greater Than or < Less Than operator makes it also return **True** if the two operands are exactly equal in value.

- The logical operators **And**, **Or**, **Xor** and **Not** are used with operands that represent **True** and **False** Boolean values.

- Logical **Not** is used before a single operand, and returns its inverse value.

- The **&** concatenation operator can be used to join strings together, and will always return a string value.

- The **+** addition operator can be used to join strings together but may not return a string value if an operand is numerical.

- Multiple string values can be specified to the **Array( )** method to create an array of strings.

- The **Join( )** method accepts an array of strings as its argument and returns a concatenated string with a space delimiter.

- The **Join( )** method can accept a second argument to specify an alternative delimiter, such as the **vbNewLine** constant.

- Expressions that contain multiple operators will perform operations in the order of default operator precedence, unless parentheses are included to force a specific order.

5 Making statements

This chapter demonstrates how statements can evaluate expressions to determine the direction in which a VBA macro should proceed.

Choosing a branch

The **If-Then** keywords are used to perform a conditional test that evaluates a given expression for a Boolean value of **True** or **False**. Statements on lines below the evaluation will only be executed when the expression is found to be **True**. The end of the statements to be executed must be denoted by the **End If** keywords on a line below the final statement to be executed. When the tested expression is found to be **False**, then VBA simply moves on to the next part of the macro.

The syntax of an **If-Then** conditional test looks like this:

If *test-expression* **Then**

    statement-to-execute-when-true
    statement-to-execute-when-true
    statement-to-execute-when-true

End If

Multiple expressions can be tested using the logical **And** operator to ensure that following statements will only be executed when both expressions are found to be **True**, like this:

If (*test-expression* **And** *test-expression* **) Then**

    statement-to-execute-when-true
    statement-to-execute-when-true
    statement-to-execute-when-true

End If

Alternatively, **If-Then** conditional test statements can be "nested" to test multiple expressions, so that statements will only be executed when all tests are found to be **True**, like this:

If *test-expression* **Then**

    If *test-expression* **Then**

        statement-to-execute-when-true
        statement-to-execute-when-true
        statement-to-execute-when-true
    End If

End If

Multiple **If-Then** conditional tests can be made to provide alternative "branches" for the script to follow.

1 Begin a VBA macro module with a subroutine that declares two variables

Sub IfThen( )

Dim Number As Integer
Dim Message As String

' Statements to be inserted here (Steps 2-5).

End Sub

IfThen.xlsm

2 Next, insert statements to initialize the variables with a numerical cell value and a default message

Number = ActiveCell.Value
Message = "Number Is Below Six"

3 Now, insert a conditional test that will replace the default message – but only when this test returns **True**

If Number > 5 Then

    Message = "Number Is Above Five"
    ' Statements to be inserted here (Step 4).
End If

In this example, neither inner statement is executed when both tests return **False** – so the default message value is used.

69

4 Then, insert a nested conditional test that will add to the replaced message – but only when this test returns **True**

    If (Number Mod 2 = 0) Then

        Message = Message & _
            vbNewLine & "Number Is Even"
    End If

5 Finally, insert a statement to display the message

ActiveCell.Offset(0 , 1).Text = Message

6 Insert a Button on the worksheet to run the macro, then enter numbers and hit the button to see the messages

Refer back to page 30 for details of how to add a Button Form Control.

▲	A	B	C	D
1	Please Enter A Number :	5	Number Is Below Six	
2		6	Number Is Above Five Number Is Even	Run IfThen Macro
3		7	Number Is Above Five	

Branching alternatives

It is often preferable to extend an **If-Then** conditional test statement by appending an **Else** statement, specifying alternative statements to be executed when the tested expression returns **False**. The extended **If-Then** conditional test has this syntax:

If *test-expression* Then

       statement-to-execute-when-true
       statement-to-execute-when-true
       statement-to-execute-when-true

Else

       statement-to-execute-when-false
       statement-to-execute-when-false
       statement-to-execute-when-false

End If

Alternative expressions may also be evaluated in a conditional test by adding an **ElseIf** statement, specifying statements to be executed when the alternative expression is found to be **True**. An **Else** statement can be appended here too, to specify statements to be executed when the expressions evaluated by the **If** and **ElseIf** statements both return **False**. The syntax then looks like this:

If *test-expression* Then

       statement-to-execute-when-true
       statement-to-execute-when-true
       statement-to-execute-when-true

ElseIf *test-expression* Then

       statement-to-execute-when-true
       statement-to-execute-when-true
       statement-to-execute-when-true

Else

       statement-to-execute-when-false
       statement-to-execute-when-false
       statement-to-execute-when-false

End If

This is a fundamental programming technique that offers the macro different directions in which to proceed, depending on the result of the evaluations, and is known as "conditional branching". When only one of two single statements is to be executed following a conditional test, VBA also provides a convenient **IIf( )** function, which has this compact syntax:

IIf(*test-expression* , *execute-when-true* , *execute-when-false*)

Beware

The **ElseIf** keyword cannot be written as two separate words **Else If**.

Don't forget

Every **If-Then** construct must be terminated by an **End If** statement on its own final line.

1 Begin a VBA macro module with a subroutine that declares two variables and initializes one of them

```
Sub IfElse( )

Dim Message As String
Dim ThisHour As Integer
ThisHour = Hour( Now )

' Statements to be inserted here (Steps 2 & 3).

End Sub
```

IfElse.xlsm

2 Next, insert a conditional test to initialize the first variable – by testing the numerical value of the second variable

```
If ( ThisHour > 17 ) Then
        Message = "Good Evening"
ElseIf ( ThisHour > 11 ) Then
        Message = "Good Afternoon"
Else
        Message = "Good Morning"
End If
```

Hot tip

The VBA **Hour( )** method returns the hour value of its **Date** argument in the integer range 0-23.

3 Now, insert statements to display the current time, an appropriate greeting message, and the current meridiem

```
Range( "A1" ) = Now
Range( "B1") = Message
Range( "C1" ) = IIf( ThisHour > 11 , "P.M." , "A.M." )
```

Hot tip

The VBA **Now** constant returns the current system date and time.

4 Insert a Button on the worksheet to run the macro, then hit the button to see the time and messages

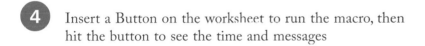

	A	B	C	D
1	9/7/2018 8:00	Good Morning	A.M.	
2				
3				Run IfElse Macro

	A	B	C	D
1	9/7/2018 15:00	Good Afternoon	P.M.	
2				
3				Run IfElse Macro

	A	B	C	D
1	9/7/2018 21:00	Good Evening	P.M.	
2				
3				Run IfElse Macro

Selecting branches

Conditional branching performed by multiple **If-Then-Else** statements can often be performed more efficiently by a **Select-Case** construct when the test expression evaluates one condition.

The **Select-Case** construct works in an unusual way. It takes a given value as its argument, then seeks to match that value from a number of **Case** statements. Code to be executed when a match is found is included in each **Case** statement.

The **Select-Case** construct will exit when a match is found and its specified code has been executed without seeking further matches.

Optionally, the list of **Case** statements can be followed by a single final **Case Else** statement to specify code to be executed in the event that no matches are found within any of the **Case** statements.

The end of every **Select-Case** construct must be denoted by the **End Select** keywords on a line below the final **Case** statement. So the syntax of the **Select-Case** construct looks like this:

Select Case *test-expression*

> **Case** *match-value*
>> *statement-to-execute-when-matched*
>> *statement-to-execute-when-matched*
> **Case** *match-value*
>> *statement-to-execute-when-matched*
>> *statement-to-execute-when-matched*
> **Case** *match-value*
>> *statement-to-execute-when-matched*
>> *statement-to-execute-when-matched*
> **Case Else**
>> *statement-to-execute-when-not-matched*
>> *statement-to-execute-when-not-matched*

End Select

A **Select-Case** construct can have many **Case** statements, and each one can specify multiple statements to be executed when matched.

Optionally, a **Case** statement can attempt to seek a match for more than one value, if the values are specified as a comma-separated list, like this:

Case *match-value , match-value , match-value*

It's always a good idea to include a default **Case Else** statement – even if it's only to output a message when the **Select Case** construct fails to find a match.

1 Begin a VBA macro module with a subroutine that declares and initializes a variable
Sub SelectCase( )

    Dim Number As Integer
    Number = ActiveCell.Value

    ' Construct to be inserted here (Step 2).

    End Sub

SelectCase.xlsm

2 Next, insert a construct to test the variable's value
Select Case Number

    ' Statements to be inserted here (Step 3).

    End Select

3 Now, insert statements that attempt to match the value
Case 1 , 7
    ActiveCell.Offset(0 , 1) = WeekdayName(Number)
    ActiveCell.Offset(1 , 1) = "Weekend"

Case 2 , 3 , 4 , 5 , 6
    ActiveCell.Offset(0 , 1) = WeekdayName(Number)
    ActiveCell.Offset(1 , 1) = "Weekday"

Case Else
    ActiveCell.Offset(0 , 1) = "Error"
    ActiveCell.Offset(1 , 1) = "Not A Valid Day Number"

Hot tip

The built-in VBA **WeekdayName( )** method returns a name of the day where weekday numbering begins at 1 on Sunday.

4 Insert a Button on the worksheet to run the macro, then hit the button to see the result of matches and failure

	A	B	C	D
1	Enter A Number 1-7 :	1	Sunday	
2			Weekend	
3				Run SelectCase Macro

	A	B	C	D
1	Enter A Number 1-7 :	5	Thursday	
2			Weekday	
3				Run SelectCase Macro

	A	B	C	D
1	Enter A Number 1-7 :	8	Error!	
2			Not A Valid Day Number	
3				Run SelectCase Macro

Performing loops

A loop is a piece of code in a script that automatically repeats. One complete execution of all statements within a loop is called an "iteration", or a "pass". The length of a loop is controlled by a conditional test made within the loop. While the tested expression is found to be **True**, the loop will continue – until the tested expression is found to be **False**, at which point the loop ends.

In VBA there are these four types of loop construct:

- **For-Next** loop – performs a specified number of iterations.
- **Do-While** loop – performs iterations only while a conditional test made on each iteration evaluates as **True**.
- **Do-Until** loop – performs iterations only while a conditional test made on each iteration evaluates as **False**.
- **For-Each** loop – performs iterations to traverse each element of an array.

Perhaps the most interesting loop structure is the **For-Next** loop, which typically has this syntax:

For *counter* **=** *start* **To** *end*

      statement-to-execute
      statement-to-execute
      statement-to-execute
Next *counter*

The counter is initially set a "start" value for the number of iterations made by the loop. An **Integer** variable is used for this purpose and is traditionally named "i". The counter value is incremented by one at the end of each iteration by the **Next** statement. On each following iteration, the counter value is tested to see if it remains less than the "end" value specified after the **To** keyword. The iteration will only continue while this test returns **True**. When the test returns **False**, the loop ends immediately without executing the statements again.

Loops can be nested, one within another, to allow complete execution of all iterations of an inner nested loop on each iteration of the outer loop.

Hot tip

You can increment the counter by more than one on each iteration by specifying a step value. For example, **For i = 1 To 10 Step 2** counts 1, 3, 5, 7, 9.

1 Begin a VBA macro module with a subroutine that declares two variables to be used as loop counters

```
Sub ForNext( )

Dim i As Integer
Dim j As Integer

' Construct to be inserted here (Step 2).

End Sub
```

ForNext.xlsm

2 Next, insert a loop construct that displays its counter value in colored cells along a row

```
For i = 1 To 3

Cells( 1 , i ).Interior.Color = vbRed
Cells( 1 , i ).Font.Color = vbWhite
Cells( 1 , i ) = "Outer Loop " & i

' Construct to be inserted here (Step 3).

Next i
```

Hot tip

This example reveals a benefit of the **Cells( )** method that allows variable values to be used to specify its row and column arguments.

3 Now, insert a nested loop construct that displays its counter value in cells down a column

```
For j = 1 To 10

Cells( ( j+1 ) , i ) = "Inner Loop " & j

Next j
```

4 Insert a Button on the worksheet to run the macro, then hit the button to see the loops display their counter values

	A	B	C	D
1	Outer Loop 1	Outer Loop 2	Outer Loop 3	
2	Inner Loop 1	Inner Loop 1	Inner Loop 1	
3	Inner Loop 2	Inner Loop 2	Inner Loop 2	Run ForNext Macro
4	Inner Loop 3	Inner Loop 3	Inner Loop 3	
5	Inner Loop 4	Inner Loop 4	Inner Loop 4	
6	Inner Loop 5	Inner Loop 5	Inner Loop 5	
7	Inner Loop 6	Inner Loop 6	Inner Loop 6	
8	Inner Loop 7	Inner Loop 7	Inner Loop 7	
9	Inner Loop 8	Inner Loop 8	Inner Loop 8	
10	Inner Loop 9	Inner Loop 9	Inner Loop 9	
11	Inner Loop 10	Inner Loop 10	Inner Loop 10	

Hot tip

The rows argument in the nested loop are numbered 2-11 by adding one to its counter value on each iteration.

Looping while true

A **Do-While** loop is an alternative to the **For-Next** loop described in the previous example. The **Do-While** loop requires a test expression that will continue iterations while it returns **True**. The body of this loop must also contain an updater that will at some point change the result of the test to **False** to end the loop – otherwise an infinite loop will be created that will lock the app!

The end of every **Do-While** loop construct must be denoted by the **Loop** keyword, so its syntax looks like this:

Do While *test-expression*

    statement/s-to-execute
    updater
Loop

A subtle variation of the syntax above is possible, to ensure the loop will always perform at least one iteration to execute its statements, by moving the test to the end of the loop block:

Do

    statement/s-to-execute
    updater

Loop While *test-expression*

A **Do-Until** loop is a further alternative to the **For-Next** loop. This is similar to the **Do-While** loop in every respect, except it will continue iterations while its test expression returns **False**. In this case, the body of this loop must contain an updater that will at some point change the result of the test to **True** to end the loop – otherwise, an infinite loop will be created that will lock the app!

The end of every **Do-Until** loop construct must also be denoted by the **Loop** keyword, so its syntax looks like this:

Do Until *test-expression*

    statement/s-to-execute
    updater
Loop

The test expression may alternatively appear at the end of the **Do-Until** loop, as with the **Do-While** loop construct. With any of these loops, the updater typically changes a numerical value that appears in the test expression to determine the number of iterations.

Beware

Ensure that the test expression in a **Do-While** loop structure will at some point become **False** to avoid creating an infinite loop.

Hot tip

The choice between a **Do-While** loop and **Do-Until** loop construct is simply a matter of personal preference.

...cont'd

1 Begin a VBA macro module with a subroutine that declares a variable counter and an array variable

```
Sub DoWhile( )

Dim i As Integer
Dim Nums( 1 To 3 ) As Integer

' Statements to be inserted here (Steps 2-4).

End Sub
```

DoWhile.xlsm

2 Next, insert statements to initialize the variables

```
i = 1
Nums( 1 ) = 100
Nums( 2 ) = 200
Nums( 3 ) = 300
```

Hot tip

This example reveals a benefit of numbering array elements to match row numbers.

3 Now, insert a loop construct that counts up to three

```
Do While i < 4
Cells( i , 1 ).Interior.Color = vbYellow
Cells( i , 1 ) = "Iteration " & i
Cells( i , 2 ) = Nums( i )
i = i + 1
Loop
```

4 Then, insert a loop construct that counts down from three

```
Do
i = i - 1
Cells( i , 3 ).Interior.Color = vbCyan
Cells( i , 3 ) = "Iteration " & i
Cells( i , 4 ) = Nums( i )
Loop While i > 1
```

Don't forget

In the example, the first loop increments the counter until it reaches four, then the second loop decrements the counter until it reaches zero.

5 Insert a Button on the worksheet to run the macro, then hit the button to see the loops display values

	A	B	C	D	E
1	Iteration 1	100	Iteration 1	100	
2	Iteration 2	200	Iteration 2	200	Run DoWhile Macro
3	Iteration 3	300	Iteration 3	300	
4					

Breaking from loops

The **Exit** keyword can be used to prematurely terminate a loop when a specified condition is met. The **Exit** statement must specify the type of construct from which to quit. For example, **Exit For**.

The **Exit** statement is situated inside the loop statement block and is preceded by a test expression. When the test returns **True**, the loop ends immediately and the program proceeds on to the next task. For example, in a nested inner loop it proceeds to the next iteration of the outer loop.

GoToExit.xlsm

1 Begin a VBA macro module with a subroutine that clears a block of cells then declares two variables
Sub GoToExit( )

Range("A1:C3").Clear

Dim i As Integer
Dim j As Integer
' Statements to be inserted here (Steps 2 & 3).

End Sub

2 Next, insert statements to initialize the variables
i = 1
j = 1

3 Now, insert nested loop constructs that display their counter values in the cleared cells
For i = 1 To 3
  For j = 1 To 3

    ' Statements to be inserted here (Steps 5 & 7).

    Cells(i , j) = "Running i=" & i & " j=" & j
    ' Label to be inserted here (Step 6).
  Next j
Next i

Hot tip

The VBA **Clear** method clears all content and formatting from a specified range of cells.

4 Insert a Button on the worksheet to run the macro, then hit the button to see the loops display their counter values

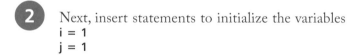

	A	B	C	D
1	Running i=1 j=1	Running i=1 j=2	Running i=1 j=3	
2	Running i=2 j=1	Running i=2 j=2	Running i=2 j=3	Run GoToExit Macro
3	Running i=3 j=1	Running i=3 j=2	Running i=3 j=3	

5 Next, insert this **Exit** statement at the very beginning of the inner loop block, to break out of the inner loop – then run the macro again to view the change
```
If ( i = 2 And j = 2 ) Then
Cells( i , j ).Font.Color = vbRed
Cells( i , j ) = "Exit At i=" & i & "  j=" & j
Exit For
End If
```

	A	B	C	D
1	Running i=1 j=1	Running i=1 j=2	Running i=1 j=3	
2	Running i=2 j=1	Exit At i=2 j=2		Run GoToExit Macro
3	Running i=3 j=1	Running i=3 j=2	Running i=3 j=3	

The **GoTo** keyword can be used to skip a single iteration of a loop when a specified condition is met, by jumping to a label inserted just before the end of the loop.

The label is any valid identifier name, followed by a : colon character. The **GoTo** statement specifies the identifier name to instruct the macro which line of code to process next.

The **GoTo** statement is situated inside the loop statement block and is preceded by a test expression. When the test returns **True**, that single iteration ends.

6 Now, insert this label at the end of the inner loop
```
Continue:
```

7 Finally, insert a **GoTo** statement at the beginning of the inner loop block, to skip the first iteration of the inner loop – run the macro once more to view the change
```
If ( i = 1 And j = 1 ) Then
Cells( i , j ).Font.Color = vbRed
Cells( i , j ) = "Continue After i=" & i & "  j=" & j
GoTo Continue
End If
```

	A	B	C	D
1	Continue After i=1 j=1	Running i=1 j=2	Running i=1 j=3	
2	Running i=2 j=1	Exit At i=2 j=2		Run GoToExit Macro
3	Running i=3 j=1	Running i=3 j=2	Running i=3 j=3	

Don't forget

Here the **Exit** statement halts the second and third iterations of the inner loop when the outer loop tries to run it for the second time.

Beware

The **GoTo** statement was much misused in the earlier days of programming and is generally best avoided. It is, however, acceptable to use **GoTo** to break from a loop iteration as demonstrated here.

Don't forget

Here, the **GoTo** statement just skips the first iteration of the inner loop when the outer loop tries to run it for the first time.

Iterating for each

In addition to the **For-Next, Do-While** and **Do-Until** loop constructs, introduced on pages 74-77, VBA provides a special **For-Each** loop construct that is useful with collections. Unlike other loops, the **For-Each** loop does not need a counter, as it simply iterates through all items in a given collection until it reaches the end. For example, all worksheets within a workbook, or all cells within a range.

The **For-Each** loop requires a variable of the item's object type to contain each item as it iterates through the collection, and the collection is specified to the **In** keyword using this syntax:

For Each *item* **In** *collection*

    statement-to-execute
    statement-to-execute
    statement-to-execute

Next *item*

As with other loops, **For-Each** loops can usefully be nested so that they can iterate through each cell within a range, on each worksheet in a workbook:

Everything in Excel is an object within a hierarchical relationship, and many objects contain collections – as described on page 32.

ForEach.xlsm

1 Create a workbook containing worksheets representing two quarter years with month and currency cell items

◢	A	B	C
1	January	February	March
2	$1,000.00	-$500.00	$800.00
3			

Q1   Q2   ⊕

◢	A	B	C
1	April	May	June
2	-$250.00	$1,200.00	$800.00
3			

Q1   Q2   ⊕

2 Next, begin a VBA macro module with a subroutine that declares two object variables
Sub ForEach( )

Dim Sheet As Worksheet
Dim Cell As Range

  ' Construct to be inserted here (Step 3).

End Sub

3 Now, insert a loop to iterate through each worksheet
For Each Sheet In ActiveWorkbook.Worksheets

' Constructs to be inserted here (Steps 4 & 5).

Next Sheet

4 Then, insert a nested loop to iterate through a range of cells to change the case of each month name
For Each Cell In Range("A1:C1")
Cell.Value = UCase(Cell.Value)
Next Cell

5 Finally, insert a nested loop to iterate through a range of cells to change the font color according to currency value
For Each Cell In Range("A2:C2")

If Cell.Value < 0 Then
Cell.Font.Color = vbRed
Else
Cell.Font.Color = vbBlue
End If

Next Cell

6 Insert a Button on the first worksheet to run the macro, then hit the button to apply the case and colors

▲	A	B	C	D	E	F
1	JANUARY	FEBRUARY	MARCH			
2	$1,000.00	-$500.00	$800.00		Run ForEach Macro	
3						
4						

◄ ► | **Q1** | Q2 | ⊕

▲	A	B	C	D	E	F
1	APRIL	MAY	JUNE			
2	-$250.00	$1,200.00	$800.00			
3						
4						

◄ ► | Q1 | **Q2** | ⊕

Hot tip

You can also use the **LCase( )** method to change to lowercase and **WorksheetFunction. Proper( )** to change to proper (title) case.

81

Hot tip

It doesn't matter how many worksheets are in the workbook, as the loop will apply to any number – try it by adding third and fourth quarters to this example.

Including with

As your VBA macro code may often want to set multiple attributes of a selected item, you are often faced with repetition that is both tedious and cumbersome. For example, you might want to set various attributes of a selected cell with code like this:

```
ActiveSheet.Cells( 1 , 1 ).Interior.ColorIndex = 6
ActiveSheet.Cells( 1 , 1 ).Font.ColorIndex = 21
ActiveSheet.Cells( 1 , 1 ).Font.Bold = True
```

Fortunately, there is a convenient **With-End** construct to alleviate this problem by nominating the common object, so you can write:

```
With ActiveSheet.Cells( 1 , 1 )
        .Interior.ColorIndex = 6
        .Font.ColorIndex = 21
        .Font.Bold = True
End With
```

Beware

You must include the **.** period before each trailing part of the chain.

You can nominate any object in the hierarchical chain in this way, so you could also set these font attributes like this:

```
With ActiveSheet.Cells( 1 , 1 ).Font
        .ColorIndex = 21
        .Bold = True
End With
```

The code may seem less readable when using a **With-End** construct, so it's advisable to indent the trailing parts of the chain for clarity. There is a performance benefit, however, as the nominated object need only be referenced once, rather than multiple times.

WithEnd.xlsm

1 Begin a VBA macro module with a subroutine that clears a block of cells then declares three variables
Sub GoToExit( )

Range("A1:H7").Clear

Dim Row As Integer
Dim Column As Integer
Dim Index As Integer

' Statements to be inserted here (Steps 2 & 3).

End Sub

2 Next, insert statements to initialize two variables
```
Row = 1
Column = 1
```

3 Now, insert a loop to set attributes in 56 cells
```
For Index = 1 To 56

    With ActiveSheet.Cells( Row , Column )
            .ColumnWidth = 6.5
            .RowHeight = 25
            .Font.Bold = True
            .HorizontalAlignment = xlCenter
            .VerticalAlignment = xlCenter
            .Value = Index
            .Interior.ColorIndex = Index
            .Interior.TintAndShade = 0.3
    End With

    ' Statements to be inserted here (Step 4).

    Next Index
```

Hot tip

The VBA **ColorIndex** property provides a color palette numbered 1-56, and the **TintAndShade** property provides lightness/darkness control from -1 to 1.

4 Finally, insert statements to move to the next column, or the first column on the next row after every eighth cell
```
If ( Column Mod 8 = 0 ) Then
Column = 1
Row = Row + 1
Else
Column = Column + 1
End If
```

Don't forget

The modulus **Mod** operator is useful for control of rows and columns – see page 56.

5 Insert a Button on the worksheet to run the macro, then hit the button to see the tinted VBA **ColorIndex** values

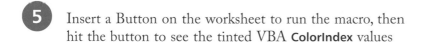

	A	B	C	D	E	F	G	H	I	J
1	1	2	3	4	5	6	7	8		
2	9	10	11	12	13	14	15	16		
3	17	18	19	20	21	22	23	24		
4	25	26	27	28	29	30	31	32		
5	33	34	35	36	37	38	39	40	Run WithEnd Macro	
6	41	42	43	44	45	46	47	48		
7	49	50	51	52	53	54	55	56		
8										

Summary

- The **If-Then** keywords perform a conditional test that evaluates a given expression for a Boolean value of **True** or **False**.

- Multiple expressions can be tested by nesting **If-Then** constructs that are each terminated by an **End If** statement.

- An **If-Then** construct can include the **Else** keyword to specify statements to execute when the tested expression returns **False**.

- An **If-Then** construct can include the **ElseIf** keyword to perform alternative conditional tests.

- The **Select-Case** construct seeks to match a value among a number of **Case** statements and is terminated by **End Select**.

- A **Select-Case** construct can include a **Case Else** keyword to specify statements to execute when no match is found.

- A **For-Next** loop performs the number of iterations specified by its start **To** end statement.

- The **Do-While** loop performs iterations only while a conditional test made on each iteration evaluates as **True**.

- The **Do-Until** loop performs iterations only while a conditional test made on each iteration evaluates as **False**.

- Two nested loops perform complete execution of all iterations of an inner nested loop on each iteration of the outer loop.

- The **Exit** keyword can be used with a conditional test to completely break out of any type of loop.

- The **GoTo** keyword can be used to break out of a single iteration of a loop by jumping over the statements to be executed.

- A **For-Each** loop iterates over every item of the collection specified to its **In** statement.

- The **With-End** construct can be used to nominate the common object in a hierarchy to avoid repetitive code.

6

Executing procedures

Calling subroutines

A VBA subroutine can contain any number of statements, which are executed from beginning to end whenever the macro is run. Execution of these statements is referred to as a "procedure".

Lengthy subroutines are often better divided into separate, smaller procedures that each perform a specific task. This simply requires the creation of individual subroutines for each task, and a main procedure that calls upon the individual subroutines as needed. This modular approach is good programming design, as it makes the code easier to maintain.

Individual subroutine procedures are created using the **Sub** keyword followed by a valid identifier name, as usual. By default, they have global accessibility status. This means they can be called upon to execute their statements, using the **Call** keyword followed by their name, from within any other subroutine in the workbook:

Hot tip

See page 88 for more on accessibility status.

CallMain.xlsm

1 Begin a VBA macro module with a subroutine that will later call other subroutine procedures
Sub Main( )

' Statements to be inserted here (Step 5).

End Sub

2 Next, add a subroutine procedure that will write the current day name into a cell
Sub GetDay( )

Range("A1") = Format(Now , "dddd")

End Sub

3 Now, add a subroutine procedure that will write the current date into a cell
Sub GetDate( )

Range("B1") = Format(Now , "mmmm d ,yyyy")

End Sub

4 Then, add a subroutine procedure that will write the current time into a cell
Sub GetTime( )

Range("C1") = Format(Now , "hh:nn am/pm")

End Sub

5 Finally, insert statements to execute the procedure in each subroutine when the macro runs
Call GetDay
Call GetDate
Call GetTime

Don't forget

Parentheses are not required after the subroutine name in the **Call** statements.

6 Insert a Button on the worksheet, then choose the **Main** procedure in the "Assign Macro" dialog and click **OK**

Hot tip

The dialog displays all subroutine procedures that have **Public** access, so you could assign any one of these to the Button control to just execute that procedure.

7 Push the Button to have the main subroutine call each other subroutine procedure to display day, date, and time

◢	A	B	C	D	E	F	G
1	Saturday	September 10 ,2018	9:00 AM				
2							
3					Run CallMain Macro		
4							
5							

Modifying scope

Accessibility status determines the availability of procedures and variables across the macro code. This is known as their "scope".

Unless their declaration explicitly specifies accessibility status, variables will by default have "local" scope. This means they are not accessible outside the procedure in which they are declared. Attempting to reference a local variable declared in another procedure will produce a "Variable not defined" compile error.

You can create a variable that has wider scope by declaring it with the **Dim** keyword outside any procedure, in the declarations section at the beginning of the module. This means that the variable will be accessible from any procedure within that module:

Dim *variable-name* **As** *data-type*

Alternatively, you can create a variable that has "global" scope by declaring it with the **Public** keyword outside any procedure, in the declarations section at the beginning of the module. This means that the variable will be accessible from any procedure within all other modules in that workbook, like this:

Public *variable-name* **As** *data-type*

The use of non-local variables is, however, best avoided wherever possible as it can introduce conflict – which local scope prevents.

Conversely, subroutine procedures will by default have "global" scope so they are accessible from any other subroutine procedure in any module. You can create a subroutine procedure that has limited scope by declaring it with the **Private** keyword, like this:

Private Sub *procedure-name* **( )**

A subroutine procedure that has **Private** accessibility status is only accessible to other procedures in the same module. It can be called from other procedures but cannot be assigned to a Button control. The use of **Private** procedures is good programming practice and is recommended wherever possible to safeguard your code:

Don't forget

Most declarations are contained within procedures. Only directives, such as **Option Explicit**, and non-local variable declarations normally appear in a macro's declarations section.

AccessScope.xlsm

1 Begin a VBA macro module by declaring two variables at the beginning of the macro code
Dim ModuleVar As Integer
Public GlobalVar As Integer

2 Add a subroutine procedure that initializes each variable
```
Sub Main( )

ModuleVar = 4
GlobalVar = 16
' Statement to be inserted here (Step 4).

End Sub
```

3 Next, add another subroutine procedure that references both variable values to display a resulting total
```
Private Sub ModuleProcedure( )

ActiveCell.Value = ModuleVar * GlobalVar

End Sub
```

Don't forget

Each procedure in this example references non-local variables, but local variables could be used instead and their values passed as arguments in calls to other procedures – see pages 90-91.

4 Finally, insert a statement to execute the procedure above
```
Call ModuleProcedure
```

5 Insert a Button on the worksheet, then choose the **Main** procedure in the "Assign Macro" dialog and click **OK**

Hot tip

Notice that the dialog does not display subroutine procedures that have **Private** access, so you cannot assign any of these to be run by the Button control.

6 Push the Button to have the main subroutine call the private subroutine procedure to display a result

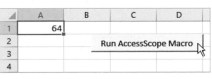

Passing arguments

VBA procedures can be created to accept arguments when called, whose values can then be used by its statements. The arguments can be any type of variable, constant, expression, or a "literal" value such as a number or a string of text.

It is important to recognize that arguments can be passed to procedures in two distinctly different ways:

- **By Reference** – This is the default way of passing arguments. Passing a variable, for example, internally passes the memory address of the variable. This means that any changes made by the procedure are made to the original variable.

- **By Value** – This is a less common way of passing arguments. Passing a variable, for example, internally passes only a copy of the original variable. This means that any changes made by the procedure are not made to the original variable.

Hot tip

The next example demonstrates passing arguments by value – see pages 92-93.

To create a subroutine procedure that accepts an argument is simply a matter of specifying an identifier name for the argument within the parentheses of the declaration, with this syntax:

Sub *procedure-name* (*argument-name*)

The argument can then be referenced within the procedure using its specified identifier name.

Unless explicitly specified, the argument will be created as a **Variant** type that can accept any type of data. It is good practice to additionally specify an acceptable data type in the declaration, to prevent inappropriate data being passed by the caller, like this:

Sub *procedure-name* (*argument-name* As *data-type*)

Multiple arguments can be specified in a procedure declaration as a comma-separated list within the parentheses, and can be of different data types, like this:

Sub *procedure-name* (*arg1* As *type* , *arg2* As *type* , *arg3* As *type*)

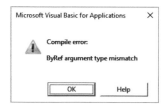

In this case, the caller must provide the correct number of arguments, and each must be of the correct data type. Attempting to pass an argument of an inappropriate data type will produce an "Argument type mismatch" compile error.

...cont'd

1 Begin a VBA macro module with a subroutine that declares and initializes two variables
Sub Main( )

Dim Number As Integer
Dim Factor As Integer

Number = 4
Factor = 16

' Statement to be inserted here (Step 3).

End Sub

2 Next, declare a **Private** procedure that must accept two arguments, of the **Integer** data type only, for reference in a statement that will display a result
Private Sub Multiply(Number As Integer , Factor As Integer)

ActiveCell.Value = Number * Factor

End Sub

3 Now, insert a statement to call the procedure above, passing two arguments of the correct data type by reference
Call Multiply(Number , Factor)

4 Insert a Button on the worksheet, then choose the **Main** procedure in the "Assign Macro" dialog and click **OK**

5 Push the Button to have the main subroutine call the private subroutine procedure to display the result

▲	A	B	C	D	E	F	G	H	
1	64								
2			Run FirstArgs Macro						
3									
4									

FirstArgs.xlsm

Hot tip

The names of arguments need not be the same as the names of the variables being passed. They can be given any valid name, but it helps to easily keep track of values if the same names are used for both.

Don't forget

This example is similar to the previous example, but happily avoids the use of non-local variables.

A VBA project can comprise any number of modules.

Adding modules

Many VBA programmers prefer to create procedures in separate modules to distinguish different types of utility, especially in lengthy complex projects. You can add further modules from the Visual Basic Editor's menu by selecting Insert, Module or from its Project window by right-clicking on the project then choosing Insert, Module from the context menu.

Subroutine procedures created in added standard VBA modules (e.g. "Module2") are accessible throughout that module and from the first standard module ("Module1"), as they have global scope by default. They do not appear in the "Assign Macro" dialog list, even though they're not declared with the **Private** access keyword.

Subroutine procedures in added modules can therefore be called just like any other procedure – unless they have been declared with the **Private** access keyword to restrict accessibility to other procedures within the same module. Procedures can be created to accept arguments that can be passed from the caller, by reference (the default) or by value, from any module within the project.

It is important to understand the difference between arguments passed by reference and arguments passed by value, to avoid errors. A variable argument passed by value can be manipulated in a procedure to produce a result without affecting the value stored in the original variable. Sometimes this may be what you need, rather than the default of passing by reference, in which manipulation in the called procedure changes the value stored in the original variable. To pass by value, you simply need to add the **ByVal** keyword before the argument name in the declaration:

AddModule.xlsm

1 Begin a VBA macro module with a subroutine that declares and initializes a variable
Sub Main( )

Dim Number As Integer

Number = 4

' Statements to be inserted here (Steps 5-7).

End Sub

2 Next, select the **Insert, Module** menu items to add a second module to the project

3 Begin the second module by declaring a procedure that will display the result of manipulating an argument passed by value
Sub CubeByVal(ByVal Number As Integer)

Number = (Number * Number * Number)
Range("D1:E1") = Array("Cubed Value:" , Number)

End Sub

The **ByVal** keyword applies to a single argument, not the entire argument list. If you want multiple arguments to be passed by value, you must include the **ByVal** keyword before each individual one in the argument list.

4 Again in the second module, add a similar procedure that will display the result of manipulating an argument passed by reference
Sub CubeByRef(Number As Integer)

Number = (Number * Number * Number)
Range("D3:E3") = Array("Cubed Value:" , Number)

End Sub

5 Now, return to the first module and insert statements to display the initial variable value twice
Range("A1:C1") =_
 Array("ByVal" , "Initial Var Value:" , Number)
Range("A3:C3") =_
 Array("ByRef" , "Initial Var Value:" , Number)

6 Insert a call to pass the variable by value, then display its current value after manipulation
Call CubeByVal(Number)
Range("F1:G1") = Array("Current Var Value:" , Number)

7 Finally, insert a call to pass the variable by reference, then display its current value after this manipulation
Call CubeByRef(Number)
Range("F3:G3") = Array("Current Var Value:" , Number)

Always remember that by default, arguments are passed by reference, so any manipulation will change the original variable value.

8 Insert a Button on the worksheet to run the macro, then hit the button to compare passing by value and reference

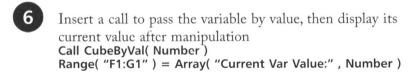

⬛	A	B	C	D	E	F	G	H
1	ByVal	Initial Var Value:	4	Cubed Value:	64	Current Var Value:	4	
2								
3	ByRef	Initial Var Value:	4	Cubed Value:	64	Current Var Value:	64	
4								
5						Run AddModule Macro		

Fixing values

Local variables within a procedure normally exist only while the procedure is executing its statements – when the procedure ends, the variable does not retain the value it contained. If you would like a variable to retain its value when the procedure ends, you can declare it using the **Static** keyword, rather than the **Dim** keyword:

Static *variable-name* **As** *data-type*

If you want to create a subroutine procedure in which all its variables retain their value when the procedure ends, you can declare the procedure using the **Static** keyword, like this:

Static Sub *procedure-name* (*arguments-list*)

Typically, the type of procedure created to retain its variable values might be passed argument values when called, to update the stored values while that workbook is open. The variables will, however, lose their values when the user closes the workbook.

A subroutine procedure declaration can usefully specify arguments with the **Optional** keyword, to allow the caller to supply or omit an argument value when calling the procedure. When this is used, the declaration must also specify a default value that the procedure can use when the caller omits an argument value:

Static Sub *procedure-name* (**Optional** *argument-name* = *default-value*)

Specifying a default argument value of zero allows the caller to optionally access a current numerical value or to update a stored numerical value:

Beware

Every argument in the argument list that follows an **Optional** argument must also be **Optional** – so it's a good idea to declare **Optional** arguments at the end of the list.

FixValue.xlsm

1 Begin a VBA macro module with a main subroutine
Sub Main( )

    ' Statement to be inserted here (Step 7).

End Sub

2 Next, add another subroutine that will retain its variable values and optionally accept a single argument
Static Sub FixValue(Optional Number As Integer = 0)

    ' Statements to be inserted here (Steps 3-6).

End Sub

3 In the second subroutine, insert declarations for two variables that will retain their values
Dim Count As Integer
Dim Total As Integer

4 Now, insert a statement to increment the first variable every time the procedure is called
Count = Count + 1

5 Then, insert statements to increase the value stored in the second variable when a value is passed by the caller
If (Number > 0) Then
Total = Total + Number
End If

6 Insert a statement to display the number of times the procedure has been called and the current stored total
Range("B1:F1") = _
            Array(Count , "Added:" , Number , "Total:" , Total)

7 Turn your attention to the first subroutine and insert a statement to call the second subroutine and pass a value
Call FixValue(Range("A1").Value)

8 Insert a Button on the worksheet to run the macro, then enter values into cell **A1** and hit the button to see the count increment and the total increase

You can declare the procedure with **Static** and the variables with **Dim**, or declare the procedure without **Static** and the variables with **Static** instead of **Dim**.

If you click the Stop button on the Visual Basic Editor menu it will reset the macro and you will lose these variable values.

	A	B	C	D	E	F	G	H
1	100	1	Added: 100		Total: 100			
2								
3			Run FixValue Macro					

	A	B	C	D	E	F	G	H
1		2	Added: 0		Total: 100			
2								
3			Run FixValue Macro					

	A	B	C	D	E	F	G	H
1	50	3	Added: 50		Total: 150			
2								
3			Run FixValue Macro					

Debugging code

It is sometimes useful to closely examine the progression of a program, by watching its execution line by line to locate any bugs. In the Visual Basic Editor you can set a "breakpoint" to halt execution on a particular line, then click the Step Into option on the Debug menu to move through the program one line at a time. When you begin debugging, you can open a Locals window to monitor the value of particular local variables as execution proceeds – such as those in the nested loop construct shown here:

DebugCode.xlsm

1 Begin a VBA macro module with a subroutine that declares three variables and contains nested loops

```
Sub Main( )

    Dim i As Integer
    Dim j As Integer
    Dim Pass As Integer

    For i = 1 To 3
    For j = 1 To 3
    Pass = Pass + 1
    Next j
    Next i

End Sub
```

Hot tip

When you set a breakpoint, a dot appears in the margin. You can click the dot to remove the breakpoint. Yellow arrows and highlights indicate the current position.

2 In the **Code Editor**, click in the gray margin against each line containing the **Next** keyword to set two breakpoints

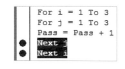

3 Click the **Start** button and see the application run to the first breakpoint it meets

4 Click **View, Locals Window** to launch the Locals window and notice the current value of each variable

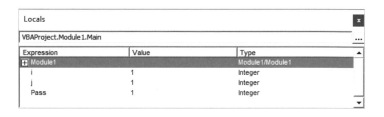

96

5 Watch the variable values change as you repeatedly click the **Start** (**Continue**) button to move to each **Next** breakpoint until you reach the third outer **Next** statement

6 Use **Debug, Step Into** to reach the end of the subroutine

Programming errors are often called "bugs" and the process of tracking them down is often called "debugging".

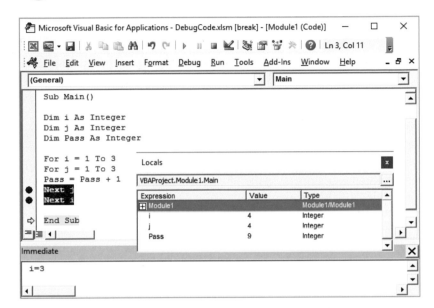

```
Sub Main()

Dim i As Integer
Dim j As Integer
Dim Pass As Integer

For i = 1 To 3
For j = 1 To 3
Pass = Pass + 1
Next j
Next i

End Sub
```

Locals — VBAProject.Module1.Main

Expression	Value	Type
Module1		Module1/Module1
i	4	Integer
j	4	Integer
Pass	9	Integer

Immediate
i=3

The **Locals Window** shows all variables in current scope as the macro proceeds.

At the end of the subroutine each counter variable has been incremented beyond the upper limit set in the **For** statements, to exit each loop, and there has been a total of nine iterations (3 x 3).

7 Click the **Stop** button to finish, then click the **Start** button to once more run to the first breakpoint

8 Click **View, Immediate Windows** to launch the Immediate window

9 In the Immediate window, type **i = 3** and hit **Enter**, to immediately move to the start of the third outer loop

10 Use the **Debug, Step Into** option to step through each line of the final complete outer loop iteration

Any code you type into the Immediate window is dynamically applied to the application being debugged, but does not change its code. Try typing **MsgBox i+j** into the Immediate window, then hit the **Enter** key.

Handling errors

The Visual Basic Editor helpfully catches syntax errors in your code when you try to run a macro, and displays an error dialog describing the nature of the error and halts execution of the procedure. For example, when it encounters an undefined item:

Ensure you verify the Visual Basic Editor **Error Trapping** settings. From the VBE menu, select **Tools**, **Options** then choose the **General** tab and be sure to check the option to **Break on Unhandled Errors**.

As execution has stopped, the programmer must correct the error before the procedure can complete. Similarly, when a runtime error occurs, VBA will halt execution and display an error dialog describing the nature of that error.

The macro programmer must attempt to anticipate how a user might cause runtime errors and plan how to handle them. If you perhaps anticipate a possible trivial error, of little consequence to the macro, you can have VBA ignore the error without displaying the standard error dialog, by adding this statement at the beginning of the procedure:

On Error Resume Next

Alternatively, a custom error handler can be created at the end of the procedure, following an **Exit Sub** statement that will otherwise complete the procedure. This will skip execution without displaying the standard error dialog. To use a custom error handler, simply add this statement at the beginning of the procedure:

On Error GoTo *ErrorHandler*

Hot tip

The label does not have to be named "ErrorHandler", but it is common practice to use that name.

Your custom error handler can retrieve the standard description of an error from the **Description** property of the VBA **Err** object, and you can extend this to provide a more user-friendly message:

 1 Begin a VBA macro module with a subroutine that declares and initializes a variable, then displays a result
Sub Main( )

ErrorHandler.xlsm

' Statement to be inserted here (Steps 3 & 5).

Dim Number As Double
Number = Range("B1")
Range("C1:D1") = Array("Tripled:" , (Number * 3))

' Statement to be inserted here (Step 6).

End Sub

2 Insert a Button on the worksheet to run the macro, then enter a non-numeric value in cell **B1** and hit the button to see a standard error dialog

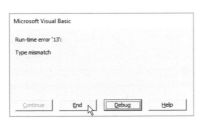

Microsoft Visual Basic

Run-time error '13':

Type mismatch

Continue   End   Debug   Help

Notice that the standard error dialog provides a button to debug the error – not very user-friendly for other users.

3 Click **End** to close the standard error dialog, then insert this statement at the beginning of the procedure
On Error Resume Next

4 Again, enter a non-numeric value in cell **B1** and run the macro to see the procedure complete – but not as desired

	A	B	C	D
1	Please Enter A Number To Triple :	Fifty	Tripled: 0	
2				
3			Run ErrorHandler Macro	

5 Edit the statement you inserted at the beginning of the procedure in Step 3 to become
On Error GoTo ErrorHandler

6 Now, add this custom error handler at the end of the procedure, just above the **End Sub** line
Exit Sub
ErrorHandler: MsgBox Err.Description & vbNewLine _
& "The Number Must Be In Numeric Format Only" _
& vbNewLine & "Please Try Again"

7 Once more, enter a non-numeric value in cell **B1** and run the macro to see a user-friendly error message

Microsoft Excel   ×

Type mismatch
The Number Must Be In Numeric Format Only
Please Try Again

OK

You don't need to display the standard error description at all, if you prefer just to display your own description.

8 Enter a value in numeric format into cell **B1** and run the macro to see the procedure complete – as desired

	A	B	C	D
1	Please Enter A Number To Triple :	50	Tripled: 150	
2				
3			Run ErrorHandler Macro	

Summary

- Subroutine procedures are created using the **Sub** keyword and are called using the **Call** keyword followed by their name.

- By default, variables have local scope and subroutine procedures have global scope.

- The declarations section can be used to create module-level variables with the **Dim** keyword, and global variables with the **Public** keyword.

- The **Private** keyword can be included in a subroutine declaration to restrict its accessibility to only that module.

- Arguments passed by reference *do* affect the original item, but arguments passed by value *do not* affect the original item.

- The **As** keyword can be used to specify the data type of an argument in a procedure declaration.

- Multiple arguments can be included within the parentheses of a procedure declaration as a comma-separated list.

- The **ByVal** keyword can be used in an arguments list to specify that the argument will be passed by value.

- The value contained in a local variable is lost when the procedure ends, unless it was declared as a **Static** variable.

- Procedure declarations can include the **Static** keyword to ensure that all its variables retain their value on completion.

- The **Optional** keyword can be used in a procedure declaration to specify that an argument may be omitted by the caller.

- Arguments that are optional must specify a default value and appear at the end of a procedure declaration arguments list.

- Breakpoints allow the code to be examined line by line when debugging errors.

- An **On Error Resume Next** statement can be included at the start of a procedure to ignore errors.

- An **On Error GoTo** statement can be included at the start of a procedure to jump to a custom error handler, added after an **Exit Sub** statement at the end of a procedure.

7

Employing functions

This chapter demonstrates how to create reusable functions in VBA macros.

Defining a function

A VBA "custom function" is a procedure that is similar in some respects to a subroutine procedure. For example, a function can accept arguments in the same way as a subroutine. But unlike a subroutine, a function always returns a value to the caller.

Individual function procedures are created using the **Function** keyword, followed by a valid identifier name that adheres to the usual naming conventions. The function name is followed by parentheses that may, optionally, contain an argument list. It is good programming practice to also specify the data type of the return value, using the **As** keyword. The function block is terminated by **End Function** keywords, and the return value must be assigned to the function's identifier name within the block.

The syntax of a function looks like this:

Function *function-name* (*args-list*) **As** *data-type*

statement/s to execute

function-name = value

End Function

As you might expect, functions can be called from other procedures within VBA code. The value returned from the function can then be used in the calling procedure.

For testing purposes, you can also call a function in the Visual Basic Editor's Immediate window using the **Print** keyword to reveal the value returned from the function.

Additionally, functions can be called from a worksheet formula, just like built-in Excel functions such as **SUM** and **AVERAGE**. There are, however, some limitations to what functions can perform when used in formulas. As a function merely returns a value to the caller, it can only be used to manipulate ranges passed as an argument, or display its returned value in the cell (or cells) to which the formula has been applied.

Typically, a function will be passed arguments from the caller, and return a result after manipulating their values, but functions can be created without arguments to simply return information.

Hot tip

Custom functions are often referred to as UDFs (User Defined Functions).

Hot tip

You can alternatively use the **?** character, which is a shortcut for the **print** keyword in the Immediate window.

1 Begin a VBA module with a function that declares two variables and will return a string value
Function SENDTO( ) As String

Dim printer As String
Dim port As Integer

' Statements to be inserted here (Steps 2 & 3).

End Function

FirstFunc.xlsm

2 Next, insert statements to initialize each variable
printer = Application.ActivePrinter
port = InStrRev(printer , "on") - 2

3 Now, insert a statement to assign the function a return value
SENDTO = Left(printer , port)

Hot tip

The property named **Application.ActivePrinter** contains a string describing the printer name and the port it is on, but this function strips the port details from the string, to leave only the printer name.

4 Open the VBE Immediate window and test the function

```
Immediate                                           x
print SENDTO
Canon MP490 series Printer
```

5 Add a subroutine that calls the function to display the information it returns
Sub PrintTo( )
MsgBox SENDTO( )
End Sub

6 Apply the function to cell **A1**, then insert a button on the worksheet to run the subroutine

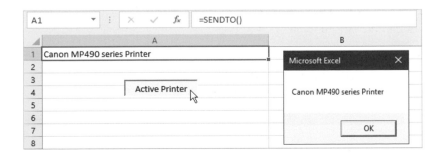

Don't forget

The value returned by this function will differ to describe your printer.

Calling a function

When a custom function is applied to a worksheet cell, it is called to supply its return value immediately. If the function performs some calculation using values contained in other cells it will, of course, reference their current value to produce a return value. Unless the values are supplied as arguments, the function will not normally be called again when values change in the other cells:

Volatile.xlsm

1 Begin a VBA module with a function that declares two variables and will return a numeric value
Function GETAREA(cell As Range) As Double

' Statements to be inserted here (Step 6).

Dim width As Double
Dim length As Double

' Statements to be inserted here (Steps 2 & 3).

End Function

2 Next, insert statements to initialize the variables with values from other cells
width = cell.Value
length = cell.Offset(0 , 1).Value

3 Now, insert a final statement to assign a return value
GETAREA = width * length

4 Apply the function to a cell that has numeric values in both columns to its left, to see the return value result

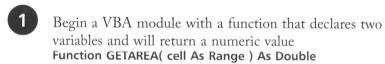

| C2 | ▼ | : | × | ✓ | fx | =GETAREA(A2) |

◢	A	B	C
1	Width	Length	Area
2	5	20	100
3			

Hot tip

Custom function names appear alongside the built-in Excel functions for quick application.

fx GEOMEAN
fx GESTEP
fx GETAREA
fx GETPIVOTDATA

5 Edit the value in either of the cells used to produce the returned result, to see the function not called to recalculate

| B3 | ▼ | : | × | ✓ | fx | |

◢	A	B	C
1	Width	Length	Area
2	5	10	100
3			

...cont'd

Not calling a custom function to recalculate when changes are made to other cells on the worksheet is probably not desirable. Fortunately, VBA provides a solution that enables a custom function to be called whenever any cell is changed:

6 Edit the custom function by adding this statement before the variable declarations
Application.Volatile True

Hot tip

Optionally, the **True** keyword may be omitted from the statement, as it is the default value of the **Application.Volatile** property.

7 Place the cursor in the formula bar, then hit **Enter** to refresh the function in the worksheet

	× ✓ fx	=GETAREA(A2)	Formula Bar
	A	B	C
1	Width	Length	Area
2	5	10	=GETAREA(A2)
3			

105

8 See the function called to produce the return value result using the current cell values

C3	▼ : × ✓ fx		
	A	B	C
1	Width	Length	Area
2	5	10	50
3			

9 Edit the value in either of the cells used to produce the returned result, to see the function is called to recalculate

B3	▼ : × ✓ fx		
	A	B	C
1	Width	Length	Area
2	5	15	75
3			

Don't forget

A3	▼ : × ✓ fx		
	A	B	C
1	Width	Length	Area
2	4	15	60
3			

You can change the behavior of this example by changing the statement to become **Application.Volatile False**.

Scoping a function

A VBA custom function will, by default, have **Public** scope that allows the function to be globally accessible to other procedures, and allows a user to insert the function as a formula. A function that is only to be used within other procedures should be declared with **Private** scope – so it won't appear in the Excel function list. For example, a function that performs a calculation when called. Additionally, a custom function can also be declared as **Static** if you want it to retain its variable values after it has been called. For example, a utility function that returns a current status value:

FuncScope.xlsm

1 Insert a range of values on a row, then add a label denoting their scale, and a button to perform conversion

▲	A	B	C	D	E	F	G	H	I	J	K	L
1	Average Monthly Temperatures : New York											
2	Jan	Feb	Mar	Apr	May	Jun	Jul	Aug	Sep	Oct	Nov	Dec
3	2	2	4	11	16	22	25	24	20	14	9	9
4												
5	Centigrade				Change Temperature Scale							

Don't forget

The _ underscore character is used for code continuation on a new line in VBA.

2 Next, begin a VBA module with a **Private** function that performs one of two calculations on a cell value argument, according to the status of a Boolean argument

```
Private Function _
CONVERSION( flag As Boolean , cell As Range ) As Double

If ( flag = True ) Then
CONVERSION = ( ( cell.Value * 9 ) / 5 ) + 32
Else
CONVERSION = ( ( cell.Value - 32 ) * 5 ) / 9
End If

End Function
```

Hot tip

The built-in **IsEmpty( )** function returns **True** when its variable argument has not been initialized.

3 Now, add a **Private Static** function that toggles a Boolean variable value each time it is called

```
Private Static Function SETFLAG( ) As Boolean

Dim status As Boolean
If ( IsEmpty( status ) Or ( status = False) ) Then
status = True
Else
status = False
End If
SETFLAG = status
End Function
```

...cont'd

4 Begin a subroutine that declares two variables
Sub ChangeScale( )

Dim cell As Range
Dim flag As Boolean

' Statements to be inserted here (Steps 5-7).

End Sub

5 Insert a statement that initializes a variable with the current status by calling the **Private Static** function
flag = SETFLAG( )

6 Then, insert statements that set the label with an appropriate value for the current status
If (flag = True) Then
Range("A5").Value = "Fahrenheit"
Else
Range("A5:).Value = "Centigrade"
End If

7 Insert a loop that converts the value of each cell on a row by calling the **Private** function on each iteration
For Each cell In Range("A3:L3")
cell.Value = CONVERSION(flag , cell)
Next cell

8 Assign the subroutine macro to the button, then hit the button to see the values and label change

Add a **MsgBox flag** statement to the subroutine to see the status value change each time you hit the button.

In this example, the code calls the **Private** function on 12 separate occasions. The next example demonstrates how this can be performed more efficiently.

	A	B	C	D	E	F	G	H	I	J	K	L
1	Average Monthly Temperatures : New York											
2	Jan	Feb	Mar	Apr	May	Jun	Jul	Aug	Sep	Oct	Nov	Dec
3	35.6	35.6	39.2	51.8	60.8	71.6	77	75.2	68	57.2	48.2	48.2
4												
5		Fahrenheit			Change Temperature Scale							

	A	B	C	D	E	F	G	H	I	J	K	L
1	Average Monthly Temperatures : New York											
2	Jan	Feb	Mar	Apr	May	Jun	Jul	Aug	Sep	Oct	Nov	Dec
3	2	2	4	11	16	22	25	24	20	14	9	9
4												
5		Centigrade			Change Temperature Scale							

107

Passing array arguments

A VBA custom function can be passed arrays as arguments, then it can process each array element and return a single value to the caller. The array can consist of a range of cells whose values can each be manipulated by the function following a single call. This is often more efficient than calling a function multiple times. Additionally, a function can be specified as an argument in another function's declaration – so the value returned by the specified function will be passed as an argument:

ArrayArg.xlsm

 1 Insert a range of values on a row, then add a label denoting their scale, and a button to perform conversion

	A	B	C	D	E	F	G	H	I	J	K	L
1	Average Monthly Precipitation : New York											
2	Jan	Feb	Mar	Apr	May	Jun	Jul	Aug	Sep	Oct	Nov	Dec
3	3.9	2.95	4.06	3.94	4.45	3.5	4.53	4.13	3.98	3.39	3.82	3.58
4												
5		Inches				Change Precipitation Scale						

2 Next, begin a VBA module with a **Private** function that performs one of two calculations on a cell value argument, according to the status of a Boolean argument, and returns an appropriate label value

```
Private Function _
CONVERSION( flag As Boolean , row As Range ) As String

Dim cell As Range

If ( flag = True ) Then

For Each cell In row
cell = Round( ( cell.Value * 25.4 ) )
Next cell
CONVERSION = "Millimeters"

Else

For Each cell In row
cell = Round( ( cell.Value / 25.4 ) , 2 )
Next cell
CONVERSION = "Inches"

End If

End Function
```

Hot tip

The built-in **Round( )** function rounds a decimal number to an integer or to the number of decimal places specified by its optional second argument.

3 Now, add a **Private Static** function that toggles a Boolean variable value each time it is called

```
Private Static Function SETFLAG( ) As Boolean

Dim status As Boolean
If ( IsEmpty( status ) Or ( status = False) ) Then
status = True
Else
status = False
End If
SETFLAG = status
End Function
```

Don't forget

The **Private Static** function is identical to that in the previous example – processing code has been moved from the subroutine to the **Private** function.

4 Add a subroutine that sets the label with an appropriate value for the current status, and converts the value of each cell on a row by calling the **Private** function only once

```
Sub ChangeScale( )

Range( "A5" ).Value = _
CONVERSION( SETFLAG( ) , Range( "A3:L3" ) )

End Sub
```

5 Assign the subroutine macro to the button, then hit the button to see the values and label change

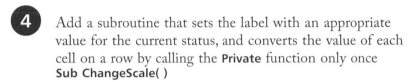

◢	A	B	C	D	E	F	G	H	I	J	K	L
1	Average Monthly Precipitation : New York											
2	Jan	Feb	Mar	Apr	May	Jun	Jul	Aug	Sep	Oct	Nov	Dec
3	99	75	103	100	113	89	115	105	101	86	97	91
4												
5	Millimeters			Change Precipitation Scale								

◢	A	B	C	D	E	F	G	H	I	J	K	L
1	Average Monthly Precipitation : New York											
2	Jan	Feb	Mar	Apr	May	Jun	Jul	Aug	Sep	Oct	Nov	Dec
3	3.9	2.95	4.06	3.94	4.45	3.5	4.53	4.13	3.98	3.39	3.82	3.58
4												
5	Inches			Change Precipitation Scale								

Don't forget

This example is more efficient than the previous example, as the code calls the **Private** function on just one occasion.

Notice that the globally accessible subroutine, which has **Public** scope by default, only contains a single statement as the processing code is hidden away in **Private** functions. This is considered to be good programming practice.

Stating options

A VBA custom function declaration can specify arguments to be optional, by preceding the argument name with the **Optional** keyword. All optional arguments must appear at the end of the argument list, after all required arguments.

You can discover whether an optional argument has been passed from the caller, by specifying the argument name within the parentheses of the built-in **IsMissing( )** function. This will return **True** when the argument is omitted, or **False** when it is present, but can only be used if the argument is of the **Variant** data type.

Similarly, a function declaration can allow an indefinite number of optional arguments to be passed from the caller, by preceding an array argument name with the **ParamArray** keyword. This must be the final argument in the argument list, and must also be of the **Variant** data type:

FuncOpt.xlsm

You can only specify an argument of the **Variant** data type to the **IsMissing( )** function.

1 Begin a VBA module with a function declaration that has one required argument and two optional arguments
Private Function GETAREA(width As Double , _
Optional length As Variant , _
Optional height As Variant) As Double

' Statements to be inserted here (Step 2).

End Function

2 Next, insert statements to assign a return value according to the number of arguments passed from the caller
If IsMissing(length) Then
GETAREA = width * width
ElseIf IsMissing(height) Then
GETAREA = width * length
Else
GETAREA = (width * length) / 2
End If

3 Now, add a function declaration that has an indefinite number of optional arguments
Private Function _
GETSUM(ParamArray nums( ) As Variant) As Double

' Statements to be inserted here (Step 4).

End Function

4 Insert statements to return the sum total of all numeric arguments passed from the caller

```
Dim num As Variant
For Each num In nums
GETSUM = GETSUM + num
Next num
```

5 Add a subroutine that calls the first function, passing one required argument

```
Sub Caller( )

    Range( "A1" ).Value = "Square: " & GETAREA( 10 )

    ' Statements to be inserted here (Steps 6-8).

End Sub
```

As the **Variant** data type can handle all kinds of data, the caller can pass mixed argument types, such as integers, strings, expressions, and ranges.

6 Insert a statement that calls the first function, passing one required argument plus one optional argument

```
Range( "B1" ).Value = "Rectangle: " & GETAREA( 10 , 5 )
```

7 Then, insert a statement that calls the first function, passing one required argument plus two optional arguments

```
Range( "C1" ).Value = "Triangle: " & GETAREA( 10 , 5 , 4 )
```

8 Finally, insert a statement that calls the second function, passing three optional arguments

```
Range( "D1" ).Value = "Total: " & GETSUM _
( GETAREA( 10 ) , GETAREA( 10 , 5 ) , GETAREA( 10 , 5 , 4 ) )
```

You can only specify an array of the **Variant** data type to the **ParamArray** keyword.

9 Assign the subroutine macro to a button, then hit the button to see the values returned by passing optional argument values

	A	B	C	D	
1	Square: 100	Rectangle: 50	Triangle: 25	Total: 175	
2					
3				Run Caller Macro	
4					

The Excel error values are actually numeric but the **CVErr( )** function converts them to more meaningful values.

The final character of **xlErrDiv0** is a zero, not a capital letter O.

Returning errors

The standard Excel error values, which appear when a formula causes an error to occur, can be incorporated into your own VBA custom functions using the built-in **CVErr( )** function. This requires one of the Excel constant values listed in the table below to be specified as its argument to return an appropriate error:

Excel Constant:	Returns:	Error:
xlErrDiv0	#DIV/0!	Division by zero
xlErrNA	#N/A	Value not available
xlErrName	#NAME?	Named item not found
xlErrNull	#NULL!	Incorrectly specified range
xlErrNum	#NUM!	Numeric value expected
xlErrRef	#REF!	Invalid cell reference
xlErrValue	#VALUE!	Invalid value

Having custom functions return an actual Excel error value to a cell when an error occurs, ensures that any formulas that reference that cell will correctly recognize the error. Additionally, you can test whether a cell contains an Excel error value, by specifying the cell address as the argument to the built-in **IsError( )** function:

FuncErr.xlsm

1 Begin a VBA module with a function that returns an error if a tested cell value is non-numeric
```
Private Function NUM_ERROR( ) As Variant
If Not IsNumeric( Range( "A1" ).Value ) Then
NUM_ERROR = CVErr( xlErrNum )
End If
End Function
```

2 Next, add a function that returns an error if a tested cell contains no value whatsoever
```
Private Function DIV_ERROR( ) As Variant
If IsEmpty( Range( "A2" ) ) Then
DIV_ERROR = CVErr( xlErrDiv0 )
End If
End Function
```

3 Now, add a function that returns an error if an optional argument is absent

```
Private Function _
NA_ERROR( Optional arg As Variant) As Variant
If IsMissing( arg ) Then
NA_ERROR = CVErr( xlErrNA )
End If
End Function
```

You would not normally return an error for a missing optional argument, but this is used here to demonstrate the returned error value.

4 Add a subroutine that writes a text value into a cell

```
Sub CreateErrors( )

Range( "A1" ).Value = "Errors:"

' Statements to be inserted here (Steps 5-7).

End Sub
```

5 Insert a statement to write error values into cells

```
Range( "B1:D1" ).Value = _
Array( NUM_ERROR( ) , DIV_ERROR( ) , NA_ERROR( ) )
```

6 Then, insert a statement that attempts to add cell values that contain errors – using a standard Excel function

```
Range( "E1" ).Value = Application.Sum( "A1:D1" )
```

7 Finally, insert a statement to display a message if a tested cell contains an error

```
If IsError( Range( "E1" ).Value ) Then
MsgBox "Errors Exist!"
End If
```

8 Assign the subroutine macro to a button, then hit the button to see the error values and message

113

Notice that standard Excel functions exist in the top level of the hierarchy, so can be referenced using the **Application** dot-prefix. The **SUM** function is used in this example, but the VB Editor changes its name from uppercase to title case.

◢	A	B	C	D	E	F
1	Errors:	#NUM!	#DIV/0!	#N/A	#VALUE!	
2						
3		Run Error Macro				
4						
5						
6						

Microsoft Excel ✕

Errors Exist!

OK

Debugging functions

When you call a function from the Excel formula bar, error messages are not provided in a VBA error dialog box. Instead, the function merely returns an Excel **#VALUE!** error value. In order to find the cause of the error, the function can be called from a subroutine to produce the VBA error dialog message.

To further debug the code, it is often helpful to insert **MsgBox** statements within the function code to display the value of variables as they change during execution. The function halts when each message is displayed so you can monitor the variable.

Alternatively, you can insert **Debug.Print** statements within the function code to display the value of variables as they get changed during execution. This displays the variable values in the VBE Immediate window so you can examine how they change:

FuncDebug.xlsm

Do not include the **Private** keyword in a function declaration if you want it to be used in the Excel formula bar.

1 Begin a VBA module with a custom function that populates array elements from a loop, then intends to return the final array value
Function FAULT( ) As Integer

Dim nums(3) As Integer
Dim counter As Integer

For counter = 0 To 3
nums(counter) = counter

' Statement to be inserted here (Step 6).

Next counter

' Statement to be inserted here (Step 6).

FAULT = nums(counter)

End Function

2 Select any cell, then type the function call into the Excel formula bar and hit **Enter** to see the function return an Excel error value

3 Return to the Visual Basic Editor and add a subroutine to call the function

```
Sub Caller( )
Range( "A1" ).Value = FAULT( )
End Sub
```

4 Press the ▷ **Start** button to run the macro, and see a VBA error dialog appear describing the error

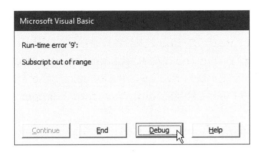

Microsoft Visual Basic

Run-time error '9':

Subscript out of range

| Continue | End | Debug | Help |

You can also set breakpoints to examine the function code for debugging purposes – see page 96.

115

5 Hit the dialog's **Debug** button to pinpoint where the error occurs within the code
```
‖ ⇨| FAULT = nums(counter)
```

6 Insert statements to discover how the **counter** variable value changes as the code proceeds
Debug.Print counter

7 Click **View, Immediate window**, then press the ▷ **Start** button again to run the macro once more

Immediate
```
0
1
2
3
4
|
```

Alternatively, you can insert **MsgBox counter** in Step 6 to monitor the variable as the code proceeds.

8 Ah-ha! The counter has been incremented beyond the final array element index number. Edit the assignment to correct this error
FAULT = nums(counter - 1)

Describing functions

Where you have created a custom function for use as a formula, you can make your function appear like the standard built-in Excel formulas by using the **Application.MacroOptions** method. This allows you to describe the function and its arguments. It also enables you to specify which category it should be listed under in the drop-down menu of the Insert Function dialog box. The category of your choice must be specified using its category number, as listed in the margin table opposite:

FuncCat.xlsm

1 Begin a VBA module within a custom function that returns a value calculated from its argument values

```
Function BULK_DISCOUNT _
( quantity As Integer , price As Double ) As Double

If quantity >= 100 Then
BULK_DISCOUNT = ( quantity * price ) * 0.1
Else
BULK_DISCOUNT = 0
End If

End Function
```

2 Next, add a subroutine to describe the function

```
Sub DescribeFunction( )

Application.MacroOptions _
  Macro:= "BULK_DISCOUNT" , _
  Description:= _
  "Calculates 10% discount for quantities 100+" , _
  Category:= 1 , _
  ArgumentDescriptions:= Array( "Quantity" , "Unit Price" )

End Sub
```

You only need to run the subroutine once to enter the function description into Excel.

3 Now, press the ▶ Start button to run the subroutine and apply the description

4 Return to Excel and select an empty cell, then click the *fx* **Insert Function** button to open the Insert Function dialog box

5 Select your chosen category to find your function listed – in this example, select the "Financial" category

...cont'd

6 Select your function, then click **OK** to open the Function Arguments dialog box

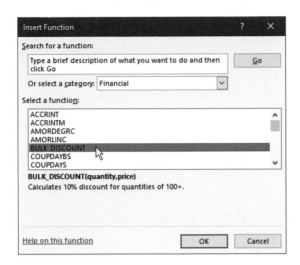

7 Enter cell references to supply argument values, then click **OK** to apply the formula

8 Drag the cell's fill handle to copy the formula to other cells as required – just like any built-in Excel formula

	A	B	C	D	E
	Quantity	Price	Total	Discount	
2	100	$5.99	$599.00	$59.90	
3	50	$12.50	$625.00	$0.00	
4	200	$8.25	$1,650.00	$165.00	
5					

D2 | =BULK_DISCOUNT(A2,B2)

Categories:	
1	Financial
2	Date & Time
3	Math & Trig
4	Statistical
5	Lookup & Reference
6	Database
7	Text
8	Logical
9	Information
10	Commands
11	Customizing
12	Macro Control
13	DDE/External
14	User Defined
15	Engineering
16	Cube
17	Compatibility
18	Web

117

Notice that your descriptions appear on each function dialog.

Summary

- A VBA custom function always returns a value to the caller.

- In a function declaration, the **Function** keyword is followed by parentheses that may contain an argument list.

- It is good programming practice to specify the data type of a function's return value, using the **As** keyword.

- A custom function can be called from other procedures or from a worksheet formula.

- Functions will typically return a value to the caller or to the cell in which the formula has been applied.

- Functions that are supplied argument values from other cells will not be called again when those cell values change, unless the function block includes an **Application.Volatile** statement.

- By default, a custom function has **Public** scope.

- Functions that are only for use by other procedures should be declared as **Private** so they do not appear in the function list.

- A custom function can be declared as **Static** in order to retain its variable values after it has been called.

- With function calls, it is often more efficient to pass a range as an array argument rather than calling multiple times.

- Function arguments that are declared as **Optional** must appear at the end of the argument list.

- The built-in **IsMissing( )** function can determine if an optional **Variant** type argument has been passed from the caller.

- An argument list can allow an indefinite number of optional **Variant** type arguments using the **ParamArray** keyword.

- The built-in **CVErr( )** function can be used to return an Excel error value from a function.

- When debugging code, it is often helpful to insert **MsgBox** or **Debug.Print** statements to examine variable values.

- The **Application.MacroOptions** method allows you to describe functions so they appear like built-in functions.

8 Recognizing events

Creating event-handlers

Throughout an Excel session, the user causes various "events" to occur by the actions they perform. For example, opening a workbook, changing a cell value, and clicking a button, are all events. Excel recognizes each event, and you can create macro code in VBA to respond to any event. It is, however, important to understand that there are several different types of events:

- **Workbook events**: Events that occur for an entire workbook, such as when it is opened or closed.

- **Worksheet events**: Events that occur for an individual worksheet, such as when a cell value is changed.

- **Chart events**: Events that occur for an individual chart, such as when the value of a data point is changed.

- **Application Object events**: Events that occur for Excel objects, such as when a new workbook is created.

- **UserForm events**: Events that occur for an individual UserForm, such as when a **CheckBox** control gets checked.

- **Application events**: Events that occur for the Excel application itself, specifically the **OnTime** and **OnKey** events.

The VBA code that can respond to these events are procedures known as "event-handlers". In order to recognize the events, the handler code must be created in the appropriate module. Previous examples in this book have been created in a "General" module, as indicated in the Visual Basic Editor window.

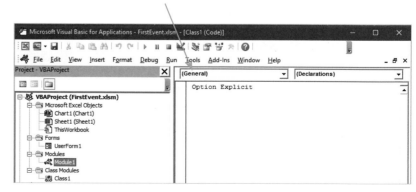

Add a chart sheet, then use the Insert menu to add a UserForm and Class module to the project – as seen here in Project Explorer.

Initially, only the General module is available in the drop-down list, until you select a module in the Project Explorer window.

1 Double-click the **ThisWorkbook** node in Project Explorer

2 Click the drop-down arrow button in the Visual Basic Editor window to see a **Workbook** item has been added

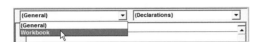

3 Select the **Workbook** item to see the cursor appear in a **Workbook_Open( )** event-handler block – ready to create a response to that workbook's **Open** event

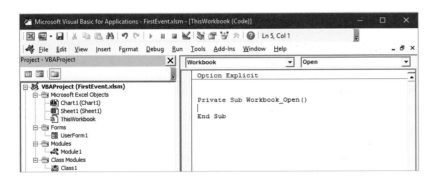

4 Double-click on other nodes to select their code module – **Sheet1** for its **Worksheet** module, **Chart1** for its **Chart** module, **Class1** for its **Class** module, and **UserForm1** for its **UserForm** module

The appropriate code module must be used to create event-handlers for these events:

● **Workbook module**: for Workbook events.

● **Worksheet module**: for Worksheet events (in that sheet).

● **Chart module**: for Chart events (in that chart).

● **Class module**: for Application Object events.

● **UserForm module**: for UserForm events (in that UserForm).

● **General module**: for Application **OnTime** and **OnKey** events.

FirstEvent.xlsm

You can also right-click on a node and choose View Code to see its code module in the Editor window.

The UserForm will open in Design view, where you add visual components. Click View, Code to see the code-behind page, where you can create event-handlers for the form.

Opening workbook events

When a user opens a workbook in Excel, the **Open** event occurs. The event-handler that can respond to this event is, unsurprisingly, named **Workbook_Open( )** and can be added to the **Workbook** code module. It is one of the most commonly used event-handlers to perform useful initial tasks, such as displaying a welcome message or selecting a specific worksheet or cell.

Similarly, an **Activate** event occurs when a user opens a workbook, and its event-handler is named **Workbook_Activate( )**. The **Activate** event is subtly different to the **Open** event, as it is also triggered if the user returns to an open workbook from another workbook. The **Open** event is only triggered when the workbook first opens.

Multiple events that are triggered by the same user action do not occur simultaneously, and the sequence in which events occur can be significant. In the case of these workbook events, the **Open** event is triggered before the **Activate** event:

OpenBook.xlsm

1. Open the "FirstEvent" workbook from the last example

2. Begin another workbook and name it "OpenBook", then open the Visual Basic Editor

3. Next, double-click the **ThisWorkbook** node in the Project Explorer window

4. Select the **Workbook** item in the Editor's left-hand drop-down list to add a **Workbook_Open( )** event-handler

Hot tip

You can use the Editor's right-hand drop-down list to add any event-handler that is appropriate for the code module that is selected in its left-hand drop-down list.

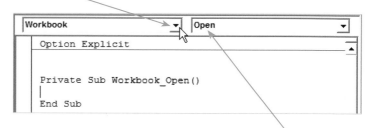

```
Workbook              ▼   Open                  ▼
    Option Explicit


    Private Sub Workbook_Open()
    |
    End Sub
```

5. See that the Editor's right-hand drop-down list now contains the name of the event for the event-handler in which the cursor is currently located

6 Next, insert these statements to provide a welcome message when the workbook is first opened
Dim span As String
If Time( ) < 0.5 Then
span = "Morning"
ElseIf Time( ) < 0.75 Then
span = "Afternoon"
Else
span = "Evening"
End If
MsgBox "Good " & span & " , " & Application.UserName

The subroutine **Sub** declarations and **End Sub** statements are not listed in these steps, as they are automatically written by the Visual Basic Editor when you select the event in the right-hand drop-down list.

7 Now, select **Activate** in the Editor's right-hand drop-down list, to add a **Workbook_Activate( )** event-handler block

8 Insert these statements to select a cell and display a message whenever the workbook is activated
Static counter As Integer
counter = counter + 1
MsgBox "Number Of Activations: " & counter
Range("B2").Select

9 Save then re-open this workbook to see the messages displayed in sequence

This welcome message will change according to the time of day and the current user name.

10 Switch to the first open workbook, then return to this workbook to see only the **Activate** event gets triggered

Notice that cell B2 is selected as required.

123

Changing workbook events

When a user adds a worksheet to a workbook in Excel, the **NewSheet** event occurs, to which the **Workbook_NewSheet( )** event-handler can respond from the Workbook code module. This event-handler is passed a single **Object** argument that identifies the type of sheet as either a "Worksheet" or "Chart". The event-handler can then test the argument to determine the sheet type.

Similarly, a **SheetActivate** event occurs when a user activates any type of sheet in a workbook. Its event-handler is named **Workbook_SheetActivate( )**, and is also passed a single **Object** argument that identifies the type of sheet as either a "Worksheet" or "Chart". This might be used to reference a cell value in a worksheet or a data value in a chart:

ChangeBook.xlsm

The argument name **Sh** is chosen by the Visual Basic Editor to represent the sheet object.

1 Open the Visual Basic Editor, then double-click the **ThisWorkbook** node in the Project Explorer window

2 Select the **Workbook** item in the Editor's left-hand drop-down list to choose the Workbook code module

3 Select the **NewSheet** item in the Editor's right-hand drop-down list to add this event-handler
Private Sub Workbook_NewSheet(ByVal Sh As Object)

' Statements to be inserted here (Step 4).

End Sub

4 Next, insert these statements to set the column width and a cell value – if the new sheet is a Worksheet type
If TypeName(Sh) = "Worksheet" Then
Sh.Cells.ColumnWidth = 32
Range("A1").Value = "Worksheet Added: " & Now( )
End If

5 Now, select the **SheetActivate** item in the right-hand drop-down list to add this event-handler
Private Sub Workbook_SheetActivate(ByVal Sh As Object)

' Statements to be inserted here (Step 6).

End Sub

6 Insert a test to determine the type of sheet and display a cell value from a worksheet or a data value from a chart

If TypeName(Sh) = "Worksheet" Then
MsgBox "First Cell: " & Range("A1").Value
ElseIf TypeName(Sh) = "Chart" Then
Dim data As Variant
data = Sh.SeriesCollection(1).Values
MsgBox "First Data: " & data(1)
End If

Hot tip

The **Values** property of the first **SeriesCollection** object in the chart sheet contains the data values from the range of cells selected when the chart was created.

7 Select a range of worksheet cell values in Excel and insert a chart, then move the chart to a new sheet

8 Add a new worksheet to see the **NewSheet** event triggered

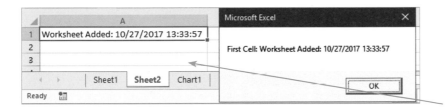

Don't forget

Notice that the **NewSheet** event has set wide columns here.

9 Switch back to the first worksheet to see the **SheetActivate** event triggered to display a cell value

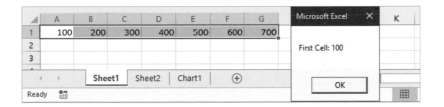

10 Switch back to the chart sheet to see the **SheetActivate** event triggered to display a data value

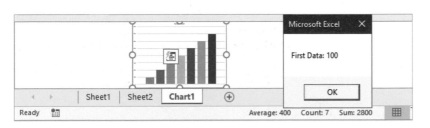

Beware

If the user attempts to close an unsaved workbook Excel displays a prompt asking if they want to save before closing – remember that the **BeforeClose** event occurs before this prompt appears.

Closing workbook events

When a user closes a workbook in Excel, the **BeforeClose** event occurs, to which the **Workbook_BeforeClose( )** event-handler can respond from the Workbook code module. This event-handler is passed a single **Boolean** argument that identifies the cancellation status as **False**. The event-handler can set this to **True** to prevent closure of the workbook if a required condition is not met.

Similarly, a **BeforePrint** event occurs when a user prints a workbook. Its event-handler, **Workbook_BeforePrint( )** is passed a single **Boolean** argument that identifies the cancellation status as **False**. The event-handler can set this to **True** to prevent printing of the workbook if a required condition is not met.

There is also a **BeforeSave** event that occurs when a user saves a workbook. Its event-handler, **Workbook_BeforeSave( )**, is passed two **Boolean** arguments that determine whether the system's Save As dialog will be offered when **True**, and that identifies the cancellation status as **False**. The event-handler can set the latter argument to **True** to prevent the user saving the workbook if a required condition is not met:

CloseBook.xlsm

1 Create a list of worksheet items that require totaling

▲	A	B	C	D	E
1	Item 1	$150.00			
2	Item 2	$250.00			
3	Item 3	$200.00			
4	TOTAL:				

2 Open the Visual Basic Editor, then double-click the **ThisWorkbook** node in the Project Explorer window

3 Select the **Workbook** item in the Editor's left-hand drop-down list to choose the Workbook code module

4 Select **BeforeClose** in the Editor's right-hand drop-down list to add this event-handler
Private Sub Workbook_BeforeClose(Cancel As Boolean)

' Statements to be inserted here (Step 5).

End Sub

5 Insert statements that prevent closure of the workbook or ensure that the workbook gets saved before closure
```
If IsEmpty( Range( "B4" ).Value ) Then
MsgBox "Cannot Close: Items Are Untotaled"
Cancel = True
ElseIf Me.Saved = False Then
Me.Save
End If
```

Notice how **Me** is used here to reference the workbook object, its **Saved** property, and its **Save** method.

6 Select **BeforePrint** in the Editor's right-hand drop-down list to add this event-handler
```
Private Sub Workbook_BeforePrint( Cancel As Boolean )
```

' Statements to be inserted here (Step 7).

```
End Sub
```

7 Insert statements that prevent printing of the workbook
```
If IsEmpty( Range( "B4" ).Value ) Then
MsgBox "Cannot Print: Items Are Untotaled"
Cancel = True
End If
```

8 Select **BeforeSave** in the Editor's right-hand drop-down list to add this event-handler
```
Private Sub Workbook_BeforeSave _
( ByVal SaveAsUI As Boolean , Cancel As Boolean )
```

' Statements to be inserted here (Step 9).

```
End Sub
```

9 Insert statements that prevent saving of the workbook
```
If IsEmpty( Range( "B4" ).Value ) Then
MsgBox "Cannot Save: Items Are Untotaled"
Cancel = True
End If
```

10 Attempt to close, print, and save the workbook to see each operation is prevented

11 Add a =**SUM(B1:B3)** formula to cell B4 to create the required total, then close the workbook

Spotting worksheet changes

Whenever a user selects a cell or a range on an Excel worksheet the **SelectionChange** event occurs, to which the event-handler named **Worksheet_SelectionChange( )** can respond from the Worksheet code module. This event-handler is passed a single **Range** argument that identifies the cell or range that was changed.

Similarly, when a user changes worksheet cell content in Excel, the **Change** event occurs, to which the **Worksheet_Change( )** event-handler can respond from the Worksheet code module. This event-handler is passed a single **Range** argument that identifies the cell or range that was changed. The **Change** event is triggered when the user, or a VBA procedure, adds, edits, or deletes a value in a cell or range. It is also triggered when the user pastes or removes formatting in a cell or range. There are, however, these changes that do not trigger the **Change** event:

Beware

Ensure the **Change** event will provide the desired functionality required by your procedure.

- Merging cells, even though some content may be lost.

- Adding formatting, unless it is pasted into a cell or range.

- Adding, editing, or deleting cell comments.

The **Worksheet_Change( )** event-handler can be used to validate values entered into a specified range of cells by the user:

SheetChange.xlsm

1 Double-click the **Sheet1** node in the Project Explorer window, then select the **Worksheet** item in the Editor's left-hand drop-down list to choose the Worksheet code module

2 Select the **SelectionChange** item in the Editor's right-hand drop-down list to add this event-handler
Private Sub Worksheet_SelectionChange _
(ByVal Target As Range)

' Statements to be inserted here (Step 3).

End Sub

3 Insert statements that highlight the entire current row and column selection
Cells.Interior.ColorIndex = xlNone
Target.EntireRow.Interior.ColorIndex = 20
Target.EntireColumn.Interior.ColorIndex = 20

...cont'd

4 Select **Change** in the Editor's right-hand drop-down list to add this event-handler

```
Private Sub Worksheet_Change( ByVal Target As Range )

' Statements to be inserted here (Steps 5 & 6).

End Sub
```

5 Insert statements that declare two variables and initialize one with a specific range that will require validation

```
Dim cell As Range
Dim ValidationRange As Range
Set ValidationRange = Range( "B1:B3" )
```

The requirement of **Set** is described on page 50.

6 Insert a test to implement validation, but only if the selected cell is within the specified range

```
If Intersect( ValidationRange , Target ) Is Nothing Then
Exit Sub
Else
  For Each cell In Intersect( ValidationRange , Target )
  If Target.Value > 100 Then
  Target.Select
  MsgBox "Maximum Item Value Is $100"
  Target.ClearContents
  End If
  Next cell
End If
```

A loop is required here in case the user selects a range of cells.

7 Select any cell or range to see its row and column highlighted, then enter an invalid amount into any cell within the specified range to see validation fail

◢	A	B	Microsoft Excel	✕	E	F
1	Item 1	$100.00				
2	Item 2	$50.00	Maximum Item Value Is $100			
3	Item 3	$120.00				
4	TOTAL:	$270.00				
5			OK			
6						

◢	A	B	C	D	E	F
1	Item 1	$100.00				
2	Item 2	$50.00				
3	Item 3					
4	TOTAL:	$150.00				
5						
6						

When the user closes the message dialog box, the code removes the invalid content and the total gets recalculated by a SUM formula in cell B4.

Catching worksheet clicks

Hot tip

To disable cell edit mode, go to File, Options, Advanced and uncheck the option to **Allow editing directly in cells**.

When a user double-clicks inside a cell on an Excel worksheet, the **BeforeDoubleClick** event occurs, to which the event-handler named **Worksheet_BeforeDoubleClick( )** can respond from the Worksheet code module. This event-handler is passed a **Range** argument that identifies the cell, and a **Boolean** argument that identifies the cancellation status as **False**. Normally, a double-click inside a cell will put Excel into "cell edit mode", unless that option is disabled. Setting the **Boolean** argument to **True** will also disable cell edit mode. A double-click inside a cell might then be used to toggle the **Style** property of the **Range** argument.

Similarly, when a user right-clicks inside a cell in Excel, the **BeforeRightClick** event occurs, to which the event-handler named **Worksheet_BeforeRightClick( )** can respond from the Worksheet code module. This event-handler is also passed a **Range** argument that identifies the cell, and a **Boolean** argument that identifies the cancellation status as **False**. Normally, a right-click inside a cell will cause a context menu to appear, but setting the **Boolean** argument to **True** will disable the context menu. A right-click inside a cell might then be used to toggle the **Style** property of the **Range** argument:

SheetClick.xlsm

1 Double-click the **Sheet1** node in the Project Explorer window, then select the **Worksheet** item in the Editor's left-hand drop-down list to choose the Worksheet code module

2 Select the **BeforeDoubleClick** item in the Editor's right-hand drop-down list to add this event-handler
```
Private Sub Worksheet_BeforeDoubleClick _
( ByVal Target As Range , Cancel As Boolean )

' Statements to be inserted here (Steps 3 & 4).

End Sub
```

3 Insert a statement to toggle the cell style of the currently selected cell
```
If ( Target.Style = "Normal" ) Then
Target.Style = "Bad"
Else
Target.Style =  "Normal"
End If
```

4 Next, insert statements to disable cell edit mode and display a confirmation
Cancel = True
MsgBox "Cell Edit Mode Is Disabled"

5 Select the **BeforeRightClick** item in the Editor's right-hand drop-down list to add this event-handler
Private Sub Worksheet_BeforeRightClick _
(ByVal Target As Range , Cancel As Boolean)

' Statements to be inserted here (Steps 6 & 7).

End Sub

6 Insert a statement to toggle the cell style of the currently selected cell
Target.Style = _
IIf (Target.Style = "Normal" , "Good" , "Normal")

7 Next, insert statements to disable the context menu and display a confirmation
Cancel = True
MsgBox "The Context Menu Is Disabled"

8 Double-click and right-click in any cell to toggle their cell style and see the confirmation messages

▲	A	B	C	D	E	Microsoft Excel	×
1	Jan	Feb	Mar	Apr	May		
2						Cell Edit Mode Is Disabled	
3							
4							
5						OK	
6							

▲	A	B	C	D	E	Microsoft Excel	×
1	Jan	Feb	Mar	Apr	May		
2						The Context Menu Is Disabled	
3							
4							
5						OK	
6							

Steps 3 and 6 in this example each toggle the selected cell's style, but Step 6 is more concise. Refer back to page 70 for more on the built-in **IIf( )** function.

The expert Excel user can still produce the context menu by pressing the **Shift + F10** key shortcut when the right-click does not produce it.

Listening for keystrokes

Excel constantly listens to your keystrokes as you type, and triggers an **OnKey** event for non-alphanumeric key depressions for which you can execute a VBA macro. These are Application-level events, so the macro code must be placed in a General VBA module.

To assign macro code to a key, the **Application.OnKey** property must nominate a key, using its code from the table below and a subroutine name – both as comma-separated strings.

Hot tip

It's simpler to use the Macro Options dialog box to assign shortcut keys to run most macros, rather than assignment to the **Application. OnKey** property.

Beware

Include error handling in any subroutine nominated for execution by **Application.OnKey**.

A key combination can also be nominated by prefixing the key code with the code for the Shift, Ctrl, or Alt keys.

It is important to recognize that the macro assigned to the **Application.OnKey** property will be enforced in all open workbooks, not just the one that makes the assignment.

It's good practice to provide a means to remove the assignment, to return the keyboard to its default status. This is simply achieved by assigning only the key code to the **Application. OnKey** property without any subroutine name. Typically, this statement can be included in the **Workbook_BeforeClose( )** event-handler.

Code:	Key:
{BS}	Backspace
{BREAK}	Break
{CAPSLOCK}	Caps Lock
{DEL}	Delete
{DOWN}	Down Arrow
{END}	End
~	Enter
{ENTER}	Enter (numeric)
{ESC}	Escape
{HOME}	Home
{INS}	Insert
{LEFT}	Left Arrow
{NUMLOCK}	Num Lock
{PGDN}	Page Down
{PGUP}	Page Up
{RIGHT}	Right Arrow
{SCROLLLOCK}	Scroll Lock
{TAB}	Tab
{UP}	Up Arrow
{F1} – {F15}	F1 through F15
+	Shift
^	Ctrl
%	Alt

1 Begin a VBA module with a subroutine that nominates a **Ctrl** + **Tab** key combination to run another subroutine

```
Sub Start_OnKey( )

Application.OnKey "^{TAB}" , "HiLite"

End Sub
```

KeyListener.xlsm

2 Next, add the nominated subroutine that will fill the current selected cell and display a message

```
Private Sub HiLite( )

On Error Resume Next

ActiveCell.Interior.Color = vbRed
MsgBox "OnKey Is Active!"

End Sub
```

3 Now, add a subroutine to return the keyboard to its default status

```
Sub Stop_OnKey( )

Application.OnKey "^{TAB}"

End Sub
```

The statement to return the keyboard to its default status would typically be placed in the **Workbook_ BeforeClose( )** event-handler, but is assigned to a button here for demonstration.

4 Insert two buttons on the worksheet to run the subroutines in Steps 1 and 3

5 Click a button to apply the assignment, then select any cell and press **Ctrl** + **Tab** to run the macro

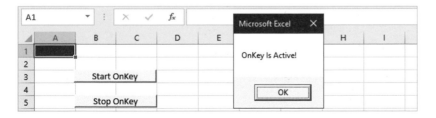

6 Click the other button to return the keyboard to its default status

133

Observing the time

Excel observes the time of your system clock, and can trigger **OnTime** events at specified times of the day for which you can execute a VBA macro. These are Application-level events, so the macro code must be placed in a General VBA module.

To assign macro code to a timer, the **Application.OnTime** property must nominate a time value and a subroutine name as a string within quote marks. Optionally, the statement may also include an acceptable delay period and a Boolean value to schedule the timer. A final **True** value (the default if omitted) schedules a new timer, whereas a final **False** value cancels a previously scheduled timer. A particular time of the day can be specified as a colon-separated string argument of hours, minutes, and seconds, to the built-in **TimeValue( )** function. E.g. **TimeValue("12:00:00")** for midday. In order to schedule a point in time relative to the current time, a time value can simply be added to the current system time. E.g. **Now + TimeValue("01:00:00")** for one hour ahead. Additionally, a particular date and time can be specified by combining a date value and a time value. E.g. midday on New Year 2018 **DateSerial(2018, 1, 1) + TimeValue("12:00:00")**.

A timer can also run repeatedly by recursively calling the subroutine in which the macro code is assigned. In this case it is important to provide a means to cancel the timer, as it will continue to execute even after the workbook has been closed. This is simply achieved by assigning the nominated time value and subroutine name to the **Application.OnTime** property with a final **False** value. Typically, this statement can be included in the **Workbook_BeforeClose( )** event-handler:

With the **TimeValue( )** function you can enter times in 24-hour or 12-hour formats – "14:30" and "2:30 P.M." are both valid values.

TimeObserver.xlsm

1 Begin a VBA module with a statement that declares a global variable to store a date and time
Dim interval As Date

2 Next, add a subroutine that displays the current time in cell A1
Sub Tick( )

On Error Resume Next
Range("A1").Value = Time

' Statements to be inserted here (Step 3).

End Sub

3 Now, insert statements to set a timer at one second intervals

```
interval = Now + TimeValue( "00:00:01" )
Application.OnTime interval , "Tick" , Null , True
```

4 Add a subroutine that will cancel the timer set in the previous step

```
Sub Stop_Tick( )

On Error Resume Next
Application.OnTime interval , "Tick" , Null , False

End Sub
```

5 Next, add a subroutine to set a timer five seconds ahead

```
Sub Set_Alarm( )

Application.OnTime Now + TimeValue( "00:00:05" ) , "Alarm"

End Sub
```

6 Next, add the subroutine nominated by the timer in the previous step

```
Private Sub Alarm( )

MsgBox Format( Time , "h:mm" ) & vbNewLine & _
"Time For A Coffee Break!"

End Sub
```

7 Insert three buttons on the worksheet to run the subroutines in Steps 1, 3 and 5

8 Click the buttons to control the clock and alarm

The optional delay period can specify the latest time at which the nominated subroutine can be run if Excel cannot run it at the specified time. In this example, it is specified as **Null** because there is no acceptable delay period.

The statement to cancel the clock timer would typically be placed in the **Workbook_BeforeClose( )** event handler, but is assigned to a button here for demonstration.

◢	A	B			D	E
1	12:17:33 PM		Microsoft Excel ✕			
2		Start Clock			Set Alarm	
3			12:17			
4		Stop Clock	Time For A Coffee Break!			
5						
6				OK		
7						

Summary

- Excel recognizes events that are caused by user actions.

- VBA event-handlers can respond to each event.

- There are several different types of events, and their event-handlers must be created in the appropriate code module.

- Opening a workbook triggers the **Open** and **Activate** events.

- Adding a sheet to a workbook triggers the **NewSheet** event, and activating any sheet triggers the **SheetActivate** event.

- Closing a workbook triggers the **BeforeClose** event, and saving a workbook triggers the **BeforeSave** event.

- The **BeforePrint** event occurs when the user prints a workbook.

- Selecting a worksheet cell triggers the **SelectionChange** event.

- The **Change** event is triggered when the user, or a VBA procedure, adds, edits or deletes a value in a cell or range, and when the user pastes or removes formatting in a cell or range.

- The **Change** event is not triggered when merging cells or when adding, editing or deleting cell comments.

- The **BeforeDoubleClick** event occurs when the user double-clicks inside any cell on a worksheet.

- The **BeforeRightClick** event occurs when the user right-clicks inside any cell on a worksheet.

- Only event-handlers for **Application.OnKey** and **Application.OnTime** may appear in the General code module.

- The **Application.OnKey** property must nominate a key combination and a subroutine, as comma-separated strings.

- The **Application.OnTime** property must nominate a time value and a subroutine name string.

- Setting the final value of an **Application.OnTime** property to **False** is used to cancel a previously scheduled timer.

- A timer can run repeatedly by recursively calling the subroutine in which the macro code is assigned.

9 Opening dialogs

Acquiring input

A procedure can acquire input from the user by opening an input dialog box that requests data entry. For this purpose, VBA provides an **InputBox( )** function that requires a prompt string as its first argument. Optionally, it can also accept a second string argument to specify a title bar caption for the dialog box, and a third string argument to specify default text for its input field. When the

user clicks the dialog's OK button, the contents of the input field are always returned to the procedure as a **String** data type. This can be assigned to a variable, but numeric data must be converted before it can be used by the procedure.

More conveniently, Excel provides an **Application.InputBox( )** function with which you can specify the data type to be returned. This allows the user to specify a range of cells, for example, and the input is automatically validated to be of the correct data type. If it is incorrect, Excel will display an error message.

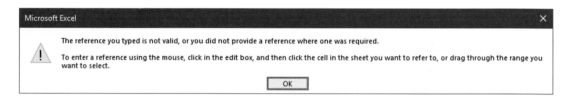

The **Application.InputBox( )** function accepts the same arguments as the VBA **InputBox( )** function, but additionally accepts an optional argument to specify the return data type using one of the numeric codes in this table. The arguments must be specified to "named parameters" of **Prompt:, Title:, Default:** and **Type:**, but only the first one is required.

Code:	Data Type:
0	Formula
1	Number
2	String
4	Boolean
8	Range
16	Error
64	Array

If the user clicks the Cancel button on an input dialog box, a Boolean **False** value is returned to the procedure. This will cause an error unless a **Boolean** data type is expected, so the procedure should include error handling to anticipate this eventuality.

1 Begin a VBA module with a subroutine that declares three variables

```
Sub Total( )
Dim selector As Range
Dim cell As Range
Dim result As Double

' Statements to be inserted here (Steps 2-4).

End Sub
```

GetInput.xlsm

2 Next, insert error handling for the **Cancel** button

```
On Error Resume Next
```

3 Now, request input of the **Range** data type

```
Set selector = Application.InputBox( _
Prompt:= "Select Cells To Total" , _
Title:= "Selector Prompt" , _
Default:= selection.Address , Type:= 8 )
```

Hot tip

Notice that the default input is provided by **selection.Address** of the current selection.

4 Finally, test that there is indeed input, then loop through the range and add together the selected cell values

```
If Not selector Is Nothing Then
  For Each cell In selector
  result = result + cell.Value
  Next cell
  MsgBox "Total: " & result
End If
```

Beware

If the test for the existence of input is omitted, validation will report an error.

5 Insert a button on the worksheet to run the macro and see the input and totaled result

▲	A	B	C	D	E
1	100	200	300	400	500
2					
3		Input Selector			
4					
5					

Selector Prompt   ?   ✕

Select Cells To Total:

$B$1:$D$1

[OK]   [Cancel]

▲	A	B	C	D	E	F	G
1	100	200	300	400	500	600	700
2							
3		Input Selector					
4							
5							
6							

Microsoft Excel   ✕

Total: 900

[OK]

Showing messages

The features of a VBA **MsgBox** dialog can be specified by adding arguments after the message string within its parentheses. These can specify which buttons the dialog will display and what graphic icon, if any, will appear on the dialog.

Button Constant:	Value:
vbOkOnly	0
vbOkCancel	1
vbAbortRetryIgnore	2
vbYesNoCancel	3
vbYesNo	4
vbRetryCancel	5

The dialog button combinations can be specified using the VBA constant values, or their numeric equivalents, in this table. For example, to have the dialog display Yes, No, and Cancel buttons, specify the **vbYesNoCancel** constant or its numeric equivalent, **3**.

Icon Constant:		Value:
vbCritical	❌	16
vbQuestion	❓	32
vbExclamation	⚠️	48
vbInformation	ℹ️	64

Dialog icons can also be specified using these VBA constant values, or numeric equivalents. For example, to have the dialog display the question mark icon, specify the **vbQuestion** constant or its numeric equivalent, **32**.

A button and icon combination can be specified using the addition + operator. For example, to display Yes, No, and Cancel buttons and a question icon with **vbYesNoCancel + vbQuestion**. Alternatively, specify the sum total of their numeric equivalents – in this case, it's **35** (3 + 32).

The buttons in a **MsgBox** dialog each return a specific numeric value to the procedure when they are clicked. This can be assigned to a variable and its value tested to establish the user's intention.

Button:	Returned Value:
OK	1
Cancel	2
Abort	3
Retry	4
Ignore	5
Yes	6
No	7

Always specify a graphic icon when calling a **MsgBox** dialog to help the user easily understand the nature of the message.

1 Begin a VBA module with a subroutine that declares one variable

```
Sub Question( )
Dim intent As Integer
```

' Statements to be inserted here (Steps 2-4).

```
End Sub
```

ShowMessage.xlsm

2 Next, request a decision input from a **MsgBox** dialog that has Yes, No, and Cancel buttons and a question icon

```
intent = MsgBox( "Do You Wish To Proceed?" , 35 )
```

Use numeric values for button and icon combinations to make your code concise.

3 Now, test the returned value and display an appropriate response string

```
Select Case intent
Case 2
Range( "A1" ).Value = "Cancelled"
Case 6
Range( "A1" ).Value = "Agreed"
Case 7
Range( "A1" ).Value = "Refused"
End Select
```

4 Finally, display the returned value itself

```
Range( "B1" ).Value = intent
```

5 Insert a button on the worksheet to run the macro and see the response string and returned value in each case

◢	A	B
1		
2		
3	Request Decision	
4		
5		
6		
7		

Microsoft Excel ✕

? Do You Wish To Proceed?

Yes   No   Cancel

Don't forget

Closing this **MsgBox** dialog by clicking its X button also returns 2, just like the Cancel button.

◢	A	B	C	D	E
1	Agreed	6			
2					
3	Request Decision				
4					

Importing files

A VBA procedure can enable a user to select a file from which to import data using the Excel **Application.GetOpenFilename( )** function. This produces the familiar system dialog that allows the user to browse to a folder and select a file. Typically, this might be a data file containing Comma-Separated Values (CSV) that the user can import into a worksheet as a table.

The **Application.GetOpenFilename( )** function can accept arguments to specify a caption for the dialog box and the file types that will appear in the dialog's drop-down list. The arguments must be specified to "named parameters" of **Title:** and **FileFilter:**, although each of these is optional.

After the user has selected a file using the dialog box, the **Application.GetOpenFilename( )** function simply returns the path address of the file, and this can be assigned to a variable. The path might then be used with **QueryTables.Add( )** to import the data. This requires arguments to be specified to named parameters of **Connection:** to describe the connection type and path, and **Destination:** to determine where in the worksheet to add the table. The table returned by the **QueryTables.Add( )** function has **AdjustColumnWidth** and **TextFileCommaDelimiter** properties, that can be set to **True** to define the table, and a **Refresh** method that must be called to display the table data:

Data files listing comma separated values usually have the file extension **.csv** or **.txt**.

FileOpen.xlsm

1 Begin a VBA module with a subroutine that declares two variables
Sub FileOpen( )

Dim path As Variant
Dim table As Variant

' Statements to be inserted here (Steps 2 & 3).

End Sub

2 Next, insert a statement that assigns a selected file's path to the first variable
path = Application.GetOpenFilename(_
Title:= "Select A File To Import" , _
FileFilter:= "Comma Separated Files, *.csv, _
Text Files, *.txt")

3 Now, insert a conditional test to display a message if the user does not select a file

```
If path = False Then
MsgBox "No File Selected!" , 16
Else

' Statements to be inserted here ( Step 4 ).

End If
```

4 Finally, insert statements to display imported data in a table on the worksheet

```
Set table = ActiveSheet.QueryTables.Add( _
Connection:= "TEXT;" & path , Destination:= Range( "A1" ) )
table.AdjustColumnWidth = True
table.TextFileCommaDelimiter = True
table.Refresh
```

Note that the value assigned to the **Connection:** parameter has two parts around a semicolon – **TEXT** and the file path.

5 Insert a button on the worksheet to run the macro, then choose a file to see the table data

In this example, a message is displayed if the user clicks the dialog's Cancel button or clicks its X button to close the dialog box.

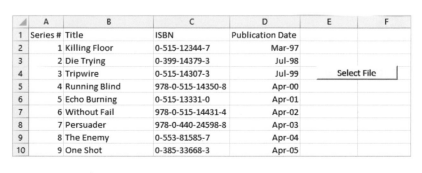

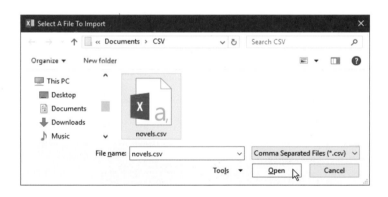

▲	A	B	C	D	E	F
1	Series #	Title	ISBN	Publication Date		
2	1	Killing Floor	0-515-12344-7	Mar-97		
3	2	Die Trying	0-399-14379-3	Jul-98		
4	3	Tripwire	0-515-14307-3	Jul-99	Select File	
5	4	Running Blind	978-0-515-14350-8	Apr-00		
6	5	Echo Burning	0-515-13331-0	Apr-01		
7	6	Without Fail	978-0-515-14431-4	Apr-02		
8	7	Persuader	978-0-440-24598-8	Apr-03		
9	8	The Enemy	0-553-81585-7	Apr-04		
10	9	One Shot	0-385-33668-3	Apr-05		

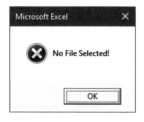

Saving files

A VBA procedure can enable a user to save a file with a name of their choice and also at a selected location using the Excel **Application.GetSaveAsFilename( )** function. This produces the familiar system dialog that allows the user to browse to a folder and select a filename.

The **Application.GetSaveAsFilename( )** function can accept arguments to specify a caption for the dialog box, and the file types that will appear in the dialog's drop-down list. Additionally, the procedure can also specify a name to initially appear in the dialog's "File name" field. These arguments must be specified to named parameters of **Title:**, **FileFilter:** and **InitialFilename:**, although each of these is optional.

After the user has chosen a file location using the dialog box, the **Application.GetSaveAsFilename( )** function simply returns the path address of the file, and this can be assigned to a variable. The path might then be used to save the workbook with the **ActiveWorkbook.SaveAs** method, or to save a copy of the workbook with the **ActiveWorkbook.SaveCopyAs** method. For example, to save a copy after importing data from a CSV file, (described in the previous example):

Excel workbooks can be saved in a variety of file formats in addition to the common file extensions **.xlsx** or **.xlsm**.

FileSave.xlsm

1 Begin a VBA module with a subroutine that declares one variable
Sub FileSave( )

Dim path As Variant

‘ Statements to be inserted here (Steps 2 & 3).

End Sub

2 Next, insert a statement that assigns a selected file location path to the variable
path = Application.GetSaveAsFilename(_
Title:= "Select A File Location" , _
InitialFilename:= "Novels" , _
FileFilter:= "Excel Files, *.xlsx , _
         Macro Enabled Workbook, *.xlsm")

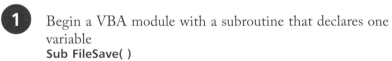

3 Now, insert a conditional test to display a message if the user does not select a file location
If path = False Then
MsgBox "No Location Selected!" , 16
Else

' Statements to be inserted here (Step 4).

End If

4 Finally, insert a statement to save a copy of the workbook in a file at the selected location
ActiveWorkbook.SaveCopyAs path

5 Insert a button on the worksheet to run the macro, then choose a location and save the copy file

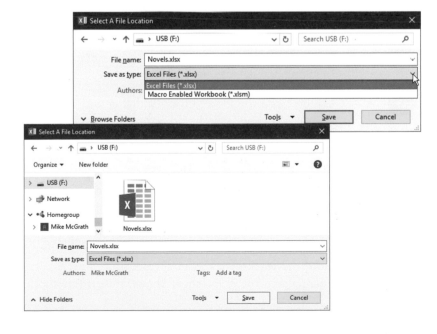

	A	B	C	D	E	F
1	Series #	Title	ISBN	Publication Date		
2	1	Killing Floor	0-515-12344-7	Mar-97		
3	2	Die Trying	0-399-14379-3	Jul-98		
4	3	Tripwire	0-515-14307-3	Jul-99	Select File	
5	4	Running Blind	978-0-515-14350-8	Apr-00		
6	5	Echo Burning	0-515-13331-0	Apr-01		
7	6	Without Fail	978-0-515-14431-4	Apr-02	Save File	
8	7	Persuader	978-0-440-24598-8	Apr-03		

Also in this example, a message is displayed if the user clicks the dialog's Cancel button or clicks its X button to close the dialog box.

Producing data forms

When a worksheet contains a table with many columns it often requires repeated scrolling to edit cells. In this situation, it can be more convenient to use an Excel data form. This is a dialog box containing one complete row of information in a range or table that can be up to 32 columns wide. Excel automatically generates the data form and displays all column headings as labels. Alongside each label is an editable box containing the data for that column. The data form has a scroll bar and buttons to move between the rows of data displayed in the editable boxes. There are also buttons to add or delete rows of data and to find data.

Perhaps surprisingly, there is no Data Form option on the Excel Ribbon, but one can be added to Excel's Quick Access Toolbar:

1 Select a range or table and ensure each column has a heading for use as a data form label

2 Click the arrow beside the Quick Access Toolbar and choose **More Commands** to open the Excel Options dialog

3 Select **Commands Not in the Ribbon** in the "Choose commands from" drop-down

4 Scroll down the left panel and select the **Form** item

5 Click the **Add** button to add the item to the right panel

6 Click **OK** to close the Excel Options dialog and see a Form button has been added to the Quick Access Toolbar

The user can now click the Form button to see a data form appear displaying the heading labels and cell data. Alternatively, a button can be inserted into the worksheet to call a VBA procedure to produce a data form, using the **Activesheet.ShowDataForm** method:

Ensure there are no blank lines in the range of data selected.

You do not need to add a button to the Quick Access Toolbar if you use a VBA procedure instead.

1 Select a range of cells on a worksheet and ensure each column has a heading for use as a data form label

DataForm.xlsm

	A	B	C	D	E	F	G
1							
2		User Name	First Name	Last Name	Display Name	Job Title	Office
3		chris@contoso.com	Chris	Green	Chris Green	IT Manager	123451
4		ben@contoso.com	Ben	Andrews	Ben Andrews	IT Manager	123452
5		david@contoso.com	David	Longmuir	David Longmuir	IT Manager	123453
6		cynthia@contoso.com	Cynthia	Carey	Cynthia Carey	IT Manager	123454
7		melissa@contoso.com	Melissa	MacBeth	Melissa MacBeth	IT Manager	123455
8							

2 Click **Formulas**, **Define Name** in the "Defined Names" group to open the **New Name** dialog box

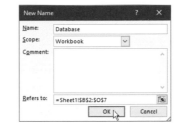

3 Name the range "Database", then click the **OK** button

The referenced range is extended automatically when you use a data form to add new data.

147

4 Open the Visual Basic Editor, then create this subroutine
Sub FormOpen( )

Activesheet.ShowDataForm

End Sub

5 Insert a button on the worksheet and assign this macro, then click the button to see the data form appear

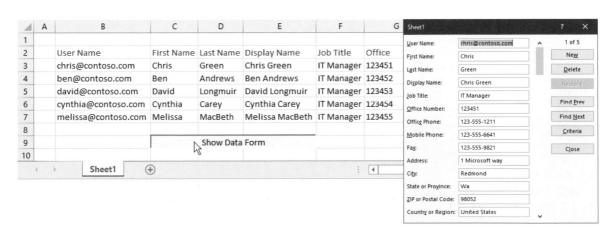

Executing Ribbon commands

Options on the Excel Ribbon execute a command when the user selects an item, and VBA procedures can also execute some commands. For example, the "Go To" dialog executes the **Goto** command, and a procedure can execute it, like this:

Application.Goto Reference:=Range("A1:A10")

This statement executes the command without producing the dialog box. Alternatively, VBA can produce the dialog box using an **Application.CommandBars.ExecuteMso** statement, stating the dialog box name as a string within parentheses, like this:

Application.CommandBars.ExecuteMso ("GoTo")

You can discover dialog names from the Excel Options dialog box:

Notice that the letter 'T' is lowercase in the command, but uppercase in the dialog box name.

RunRibbon.xlsm

1 Click **File**, **Options**, **Customize Ribbon**, then select **Main Tabs** in the "Choose commands from" drop-down

2 Next, expand the **Number** and **Number Format** nodes

3 Place the cursor over the **More Number Formats** item to reveal the dialog name – **NumberFormatsDialog**

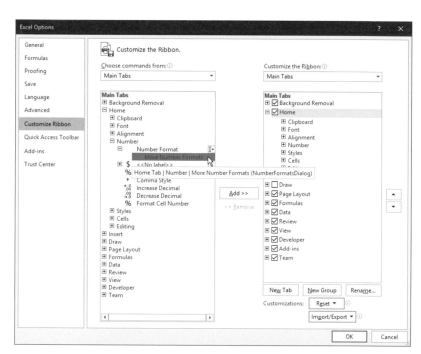

4 Open the Visual Basic Editor, then create this subroutine
Sub RunRibbon( )

On Error Resume Next
Application.CommandBars.ExecuteMso _
("NumberFormatsDialog")

End Sub

5 Insert a button on the worksheet and assign this macro

6 Select cells with numeric values for formatting, then click the button to run the procedure

Beware

This procedure must include error handling to avoid an Excel error that will occur if executed when an item other than a worksheet cell, such as a chart, is selected.

	A	B	C	D	E	F	G	H	I
1	100	200	300	400	500	600	700	800	900
2									
3					Run Ribbon Command				
4									
5									

7 Choose a format, then click the **OK** button to close the dialog box and apply that format to the selected cells

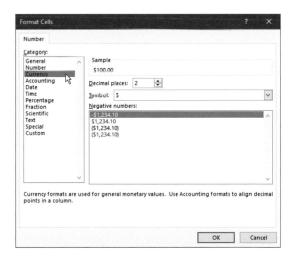

Don't forget

No value is returned to the procedure from this dialog box.

	A	B	C	D	E	F	G	H	I
1	$100.00	$200.00	$300.00	$400.00	$500.00	$600.00	$700.00	$800.00	$900.00
2									
3					Run Ribbon Command				
4									
5									

Summary

- The VBA **InputBox( )** function can be used to acquire user input, but it always returns a **String** data type.

- The Excel **Application.InputBox( )** function can be used to acquire user input and return a specified data type.

- Data type validation is automatically implemented by using the Excel **Application.InputBox( )** function.

- The buttons and icons on a **MsgBox** dialog can be specified using VBA constant values or numeric values.

- A button and icon combination on a **MsgBox** dialog can be specified using the **+** operator or a total of numeric values.

- The buttons in a **MsgBox** dialog each return a specific numeric value to the procedure when they are clicked.

- The Excel **Application.GetOpenFilename( )** function allows the user to select a file and returns its path address.

- Comma-separated values contained in a file can be imported into an Excel table by the **QueryTables.Add( )** function.

- The Excel **Application.GetSaveAsFilename( )** function allows the user to select a file location and returns its path address.

- The **ActiveWorkbook.SaveAs** method saves the workbook, but the **ActiveWorkbook.SaveCopyAs** method saves a copy of it.

- An Excel data form is useful when editing a range or table that has many columns, up to a maximum of 32.

- A **Form** button can be added to the Quick Access Toolbar so the user can edit data with a data form.

- Naming a range or table "Database" allows VBA to produce a data form using the **Activesheet.ShowDataForm** method.

- A VBA procedure can directly execute some Ribbon commands, such as the **Application.Goto** command.

- A VBA procedure can produce dialog boxes by stating their name in an **Application.CommandBars.ExecuteMso** statement.

10 Providing UserForm dialogs

Inserting a UserForm

The Visual Basic Editor makes it simple to create your own custom dialog boxes by adding one, or more, UserForms so the user may interact with the workbook:

FirstUserForm.xlsm

1 Open the Visual Basic Editor, then select **Insert**, **UserForm** from the menu

2 In Project Explorer, see that a **Forms** folder gets added to the project, containing a UserForm node named "UserForm1"

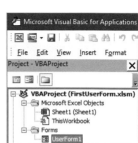

3 Double-click on the UserForm node to see an empty dialog form appear in "Design View"

The Toolbox may automatically appear when you enter the Design View.

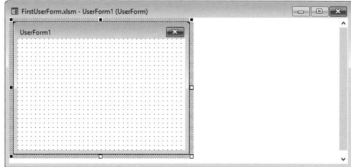

Design View is where you create the custom dialog box by adding visual "Controls" to the empty UserForm.

Position the cursor over any Control in the Toolbox to see its name appear on a Tooltip.

4 Select **View**, **Toolbox** from the menu to see the range of Controls that can be added to the empty UserForm

...cont'd

5 Select **View**, **Code** on the menu to see the "code-behind" page where you can add functional code for the UserForm

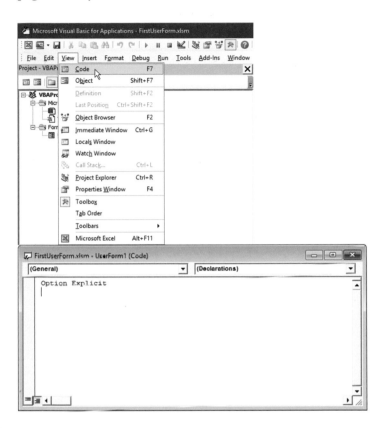

You can resize the windows to see both Design and Code views at the same time.

6 Click the ▶ **Run** button, or press **F5**, to switch to Excel and see the UserForm appear

The UserForm is not very useful until you add Controls and functional code. It cannot be resized or minimized – it can merely be moved around the screen and closed.

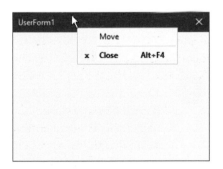

The caption on the UserForm title bar is initially that of its node – but it can be changed to be more meaningful.

7 Click the **X** button on the UserForm to stop it running and return to the Visual Basic Editor

153

Adding controls

The Visual Basic Editor's Toolbox contains all the Controls you can add to a UserForm when designing a custom dialog box. It can be resized to display the controls horizontally or vertically:

The arrow item in the Toolbox simply changes the cursor back to normal functionality so you can select objects in the Design view window.

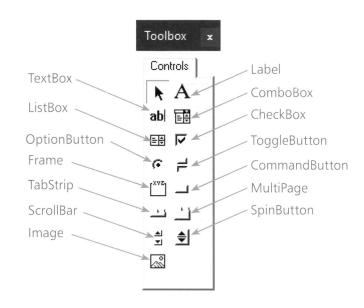

TextBox
ListBox
OptionButton
Frame
TabStrip
ScrollBar
Image

Label
ComboBox
CheckBox
ToggleButton
CommandButton
MultiPage
SpinButton

FormControls.xlsm

There are two possible ways to add a Control to the UserForm:

1 Click a Control item in the Toolbox, then drag it onto the UserForm to see an outline of the Control at its default size

2 Release the mouse button to see the Control appear, surrounded by "grab handles" – while the Control is selected

To move a Control, first select it then position the cursor over its border and drag the Control.

3 Drag any of the grab handles in any direction to resize the Control to the desired size

Or...

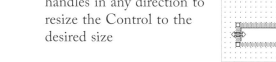

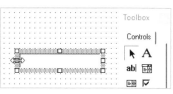

154

1 Click a Control item in the Toolbox

2 Drag the cursor across the UserForm to the size you require

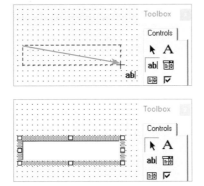

3 Release the mouse button to see the Control appear with grab handles – while the Control is selected

The cursor changes when you click an item in the Toolbox to show it is "loaded" with a Control. It reverts to normal when the item is deselected after addition to the UserForm, or if you click the arrow button in the Toolbox.

The grab handles disappear when the Control is deselected but will reappear when it is selected again. When you hit the **Run** button, the Control appears as a familiar Windows component. The UserForm illustrated below contains one example of each available Control:

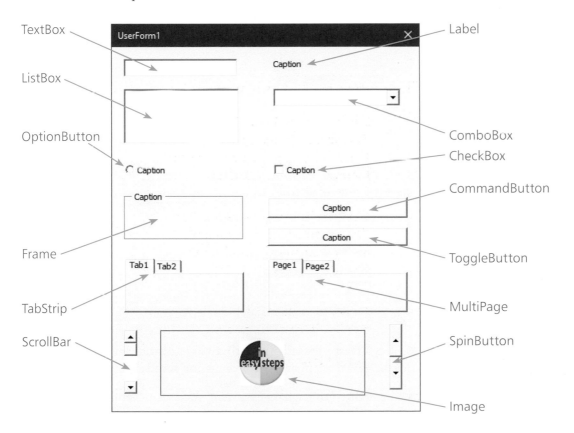

Comparing control types

UserForm controls allow the user to easily interact with worksheet data and VBA macro code. Here is a brief description of each control for comparison of how they can be used:

- **Label** – Displays descriptive text that the user cannot edit. Identifies the purpose of a field or provides instructions.

- **TextBox** – A rectangular box in which the user can view, enter or edit text.

- **ListBox** – Displays a list of one or more items of text from which a user can choose. There are three types of ListBox:

  1) **Single-selection** – Allows the user to choose only one item in the list.

  2) **Multiple-selection** – Allows the user to select one item or multiple adjacent items in the list.

  3) **Extended-selection** – Allows the user to select one item or multiple items from anywhere in the list.

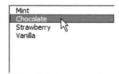

- **ComboBox** – Combines a TextBox and ListBox to provide a drop-down list from which the user can choose one item.

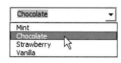

- **ScrollBar** – Scrolls through a range of values when the user clicks the scroll arrows or drags the scroll box.

- **SpinButton** – Changes a value such as a number, time or date. The value is increased when the user clicks its Up arrow and decreased when the user clicks its Down arrow.

A TextBox control may also present read-only information.

For large lists, a ComboBox is more compact than a ListBox.

- **Frame** – A rectangular control with an optional label that visually groups together related controls for clarity.

- **OptionButton** – Allows the user to choose a single item from a mutually exclusive group of options that is often displayed in a Frame control. Selecting an OptionButton turns it On and turns Off all other buttons in the group.

The OptionButton controls are also known as "radio buttons".

- **CheckBox** – Allows the user to choose one or more items in a group of options that is often displayed in a Frame control. Selecting a CheckBox turns it On and has no effect on other buttons in the group. Deselecting a CheckBox turns it Off.

- **CommandButton** – Runs a procedure that performs an action when the user clicks it.

- **ToggleButton** – Indicates an On or Off state. The button alternates between states when it is clicked by the user.

- **MultiPage** – Provides the ability to create tabbed dialog boxes with separate controls arranged on separate pages. Choosing a tab shows that page alone and hides others.

- **TabStrip** – Provides the ability to tab through data within the same controls. It does not have separate pages.

- **Image** – Embeds a picture such as a bitmap, JPEG or GIF file for display on the UserForm.

The CommandButton controls are also known as "push buttons".

Adjusting properties

Each control that can be added to a UserForm has a large number of properties that determine its appearance and performance. The Visual Basic Editor provides a Properties Window, in which you can examine and change the value of a property for the item currently selected in Design View. The Properties Window has tabs that list the properties alphabetically and by category, showing the property name and its current value. Control property values can be changed by directly editing the current value in the Properties Window. For example, with items that have a Caption property, you can simply type in a new value:

Properties.xlsm

1 Select the **UserForm** item itself in Design View

2 Click the **View**, **Properties Window** menu, or press **F4**, to open the Properties Window

3 Select the **Caption** property and type "Select Flavor" to change the text on the UserForm's title bar

Hot tip

Some Properties launch a dialog in order to change their value. The Font property opens a Font selection dialog, and the Picture property launches a Load Picture dialog.

Beware

If multiple items are selected, the Properties Window will only display their common properties.

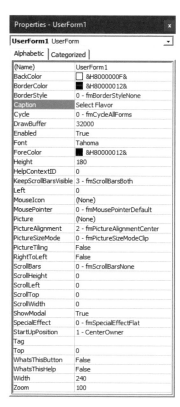

The text on the title bar changes on the UserForm in Design View as you type.

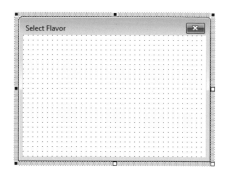

Properties can also be changed at runtime by VBA macro code. For example, items that contain a list can be populated when the UserForm first opens, by adding statements for its **Initialize** event.

158

4 Add a **ListBox** control to the UserForm in Design View – by default this will be named "ListBox1"

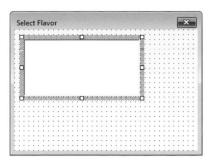

5 Next, select the **View**, **Code** menu to open the UserForm's code-behind page

6 Select the **UserForm** item in the Editor's left-hand drop-down list, and the **Initialize** item in its right-hand drop-down list – to add a **UserForm_Initialize( )** event-handler

You must have the UserForm's node selected in Project Explorer to access its code module.

7 Now, insert these statements to populate the ListBox control with four items
```
With ListBox1
  .AddItem "Mint"
  .AddItem "Chocolate"
  .AddItem "Strawberry"
  .AddItem "Vanilla"
End With
```

Avoid typing multiple **ListBox1.AddItem** statements by using the **With** keyword – but remember to type a period before each **AddItem** statement.

8 Finally, click the ▷ **Run** button to see the UserForm appear displaying your Caption and listed items

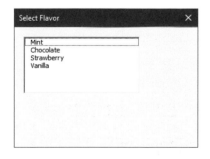

Naming controls

UserForm controls are assigned default names as you add them to a form in Design View, together with a sequential number. For example, the first CommandButton added will be named "CommandButton1", the second CommandButton added will be named "CommandButton2", and so on. It is, however, good programming practice to assign more meaningful names to each control so its purpose is easily recognizable in VBA code. For example, you may want to ensure that a particular CheckBox control is checked with this statement:

CheckBox2.Value = True

But by assigning a meaningful name, such as "chkAsia", the statement becomes much clearer as:

chkAsia.Value = True

Now the name describes its purpose, and its prefix describes its control type. The table below lists suggested prefixes for each type of control, together with an example control name:

Hot tip

If you create an application with multiple UserForms it is useful to give the forms meaningful names.

Control:	Prefix:	Example:
CheckBox	chk	chkAsia
ComboBox	cbo	cboFlavors
CommandButton	cmd	cmdAgree
Frame	fra	fraTypes
Image	img	imgLogo
Label	lbl	lblName
ListBox	lst	lstCities
MultiPage	mul	mulPages
OptionButton	opt	optMint
ScrollBar	scr	scrMore
SpinButton	spn	spnQuantity
TabStrip	tab	tabTabs
TextBox	txt	txtName
ToggleButton	tog	togStatus
UserForm	frm	frmMain

...cont'd

1 Add three **CheckBox** controls to a UserForm

2 Open the Properties Window, then edit the form and controls' **Caption** property, like this:

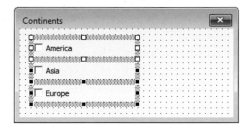

To align the CheckBox controls, select all three then set their Left property value.

3 Next, edit each CheckBox control's **Name** property to assign it their respective caption, prefixed by "chk"

4 Now, select the **View, Code** menu to open the UserForm's code-behind page

5 Select the **UserForm** item in the Editor's left-hand drop-down list and the **Initialize** item in its right-hand drop-down list – to add a **UserForm_Initialize( )** event-handler

6 Inside the event-handler code block, type "Me.chk" to see IntelliSense list all control items with the "chk" prefix

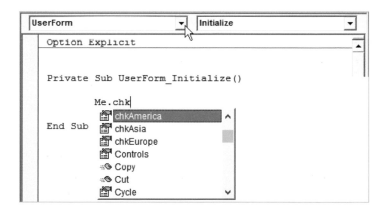

The **Me** keyword refers to the UserForm, so you could alternatively type the form's name followed by a period. IntelliSense lists all the form's properties and controls, but also typing a prefix reduces the list.

7 Select the second item, then complete the statement **Me.chkAsia.Value = True**

Do not put the procedure to show a form inside the UserForm's code module – it must be in a General VBA code module.

Don't forget

A hidden form can be displayed by calling its **Show** method.

ShowForm.xlsm

Displaying forms

To display a UserForm you must create a procedure within a General VBA code module to implement its **Show** method. This is simply dot-suffixed to the form's assigned name in a statement. For example, for a UserForm named "MyForm" as **MyForm.Show**. When a UserForm is displayed, it is "modal" by default. This means the user must close the form before they can continue working on a worksheet. You can change this by adding the **vbModeless** constant when calling its **Show** method. For example, with **MyForm.Show vbModeless**.

To close a UserForm, the statement does not implement a **Close** command, as you might expect, but requires the **Unload** method. This appears before a space and the form's assigned name in a statement. For example, as **Unload MyForm**. This unloads the UserForm from computer memory. Conversely, there is a **Load** method, which will load a UserForm into memory. For example, **Load MyForm** will load a form into memory – but not display it when the form's **Show** method is called. This is only useful if the UserForm is complex, and thus takes a while to initialize.

More usefully, you can call a UserForm's **Hide** method to remove it from display, but keep it loaded in memory. For example, with **MyForm.Hide** your code still has access to the properties of the controls on the form.

A UserForm can be opened in response to an event, such as the **Click** event of a button on a worksheet or a Workbook's **Open** event. For example, a form could be used as a "splash screen" to display briefly when a workbook is first opened:

1 Add some controls to a UserForm, such as an **Image** control and a **Label** control

2 Rename the form to become "frmSplash"

3 Next, select the **View, Code** menu to open the UserForm's code-behind page and add this timer procedure
Private Sub UserForm_Initialize( )

Application.OnTime Now + _
TimeSerial(0 , 0 , 5) , "CloseSplash"

End Sub

You can right-click on a node in Project Explorer and choose **View Code** in the context menu to open its code module.

4 Next, go to the code module of the **ThisWorkbook** node and add this procedure to show the UserForm
Private Sub Workbook_Open( )

frmSplash.Show

End Sub

5 Finally, insert a General VBA code module into the project and add this procedure to close the UserForm
Private Sub CloseSplash( )

Unload frmSplash

End Sub

163

6 Save the Workbook, then reopen it to see the UserForm appear for five seconds, centered over the Excel window

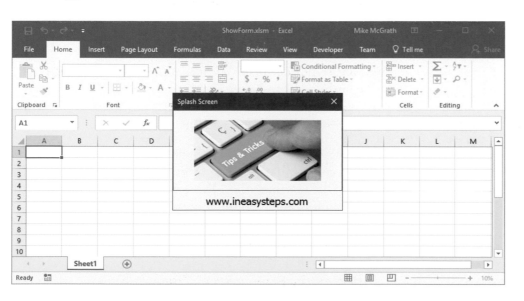

Handling form events

A UserForm, and every control on it, recognizes events that are triggered by user actions, and you can create macro code in VBA to respond to any event. For example, when the user pushes a CommandButton control, a **Click** event occurs, to which you can create a response in an event-handler.

Each control recognizes many events, which you can easily discover in the Visual Basic Editor window:

1 Add a **CommandButton** control onto a UserForm

2 Double-click on the **CommandButton** control in Design View – to open the code-behind page with the cursor inside a generated **Click( )** event-handler code block

3 Next, click the down arrow button to open the right-hand drop-down list

4 Now, scroll down the list to discover all events for this control

Beware

Some actions cause more than one event to occur. Ensure you add code into the appropriate event-handler procedure.

The same technique can be used to discover the events recognized by any UserForm control, and you can select any event in the drop-down list to generate an associated event-handler code block.

One control that always needs event-handler code is the SpinButton control that simply provides Up and Down arrow buttons that the user may click. Whenever either button gets clicked, the SpinButton control's **Change** event is triggered. In order to make this control useful, code can be created in its event-handler to respond to the user action.

1 Add a **TextBox** and **SpinButton** to a UserForm, then name them "txtNum" and "spnNum" respectively

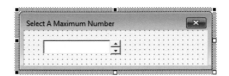

FormEvents.xlsm

2 Select the **SpinButton** control, then open the Properties Window and set its **Value** to 1 and its **Min** property to 1

Hot tip

Alternatively, set these properties in code with **spnNum.Value = 1** and **spnNum.Min = 1**.

3 Next, double-click the **SpinButton** to open the code-behind page, and add this event-handler code to respond when the user clicks its Up or Down arrow buttons

```
Private Sub spnNum_Change( )

txtNum.Value = spnNum.Value

End Sub
```

4 Now, add this event-handler code to respond when the user enters a value into the **TextBox** control directly

```
Private Sub txtNum_Change( )

If txtNum.Value = "" Then
Exit Sub
ElseIf IsNumeric( txtNum.Value ) _
  And ( txtNum.Value > 0 ) Then
spnNum.Value = txtNum.Value
Else
MsgBox "Please Select A Positive Integer" , 16
txtNum.Value = spnNum.Value
End If

End Sub
```

Hot tip

This example keeps the SpinButton and TextBox values synchronized and exits if the user simply clears the TextBox. It displays a dialog message if the user enters an invalid value, then displays the previous value in the TextBox once more.

165

5 Click the **Run** button, and change the **TextBox** control's content directly or with the **SpinButton** control

Managing lists

The ListBox and ComboBox controls are unlike other UserForm controls, as they accept multiple values to populate their lists. Typically, this is achieved in VBA code using their **AddItem** method. Alternatively, a list can be populated simply by assigning an array to the **List** property of a ListBox or ComboBox control.

Each item in a list has an index number so an item can be selected by assigning its number to the **ListIndex** property. This property therefore contains the index number of the currently selected list item.

The **RemoveItem** method can remove an existing item from a list, and can remove the currently selected item by specifying its **ListIndex** property. This may produce an error if attempting to remove an item from an empty list, so it's worth testing for empty lists to avoid this.

The **AddItem** method is demonstrated in the example on page 159.

FormList.xlsm

1 Create some string content on the first row of the worksheet that can be imported into a **ListBox** control

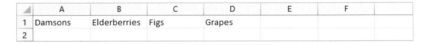

	A	B	C	D	E	F	
1	Damsons	Elderberries	Figs	Grapes			
2							

2 Open the Visual Basic Editor and add two **ListBox** controls and two **CommandButton** controls to a UserForm

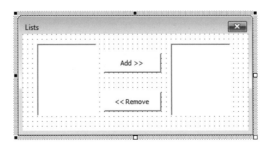

3 Open the Properties Window and edit the **Caption** property of each CommandButton control to resemble the image above

4 In the Properties Window, name the controls respectively: "lstFruit", "lstBasket", "cmdAdd", and "cmdRemove"

5 Open the form's code-behind page and begin its **Initialize( )** event-handler by populating a ListBox with three items

```
Private Sub UserForm_Initialize( )
lstFruit.List = Array( "Apples" , "Bananas" , "Cherries" )

' Statements to be inserted here (Step 6).

End Sub
```

6 Insert statements to declare two variables and add more items to the ListBox

```
Dim cell As Range
Dim rng As Range
Set rng = Range( "A1" ).CurrentRegion
For Each cell In rng
lstFruit.AddItem cell.Value
Next cell
```

The **CurrentRegion** property is the range bounded by any combination of blank rows and blank columns.

7 Next, add a **Click( )** event-handler for a CommandButton – to move items from the populated ListBox

```
Private Sub cmdAdd_Click( )
If lstFruit.Value <> "" Then
lstBasket.AddItem lstFruit.Value
lstFruit.RemoveItem listFruit.ListIndex
End If
End Sub
```

167

8 Now, add a **Click( )** event handler for a CommandButton – to return items to the populated ListBox

```
Private Sub cmdRemove_Click( )
If lstBasket.Value <> "" Then
lstFruit.AddItem lstBasket.Value
lstBasket.RemoveItem listBasket.ListIndex
End If
End Sub
```

The value "" is two double quote marks that represent an empty list.

9 Run the macro, then click the CommandButton controls to manage the lists

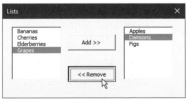
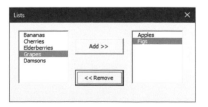

Summary

- A **UserForm** is a custom dialog box that allows the user to interact with the Excel workbook.

- Functional code must be added to a UserForm's code-behind page to make the form useful.

- All visual controls that can be added to a UserForm are contained in the Visual Basic Editor's **Toolbox**.

- Controls are added to a UserForm in **Design View**, and can be resized by dragging their grab handles.

- A **ListBox** control can allow single selection, multiple selection, or extended selection of list items.

- An **OptionButton** control allows the user to select one item in a group, but a **CheckBox** control allows multiple selections.

- The **Properties Window** lists all properties of a selected control alphabetically and by category.

- Control property values can be changed directly in the Properties Window at designtime or in code at runtime.

- It is good practice to rename controls with meaningful names, so their purpose is easily recognizable in VBA code.

- A UserForm opens when its **Show** method is called, and closes when its **Unload** method is called.

- By default, a UserForm is modal, so the user cannot continue working on a worksheet until the form has been closed.

- A UserForm and all controls on it recognize events that are triggered by user actions on the form.

- Event-handler procedures can respond to UserForm events, and a **SpinButton** control will always need an event-handler.

- Unlike other controls, the **ListBox** and **ComboBox** controls accept multiple values to populate their lists.

- List controls can be populated using the control's **AddItem** method, or by assigning an array to their **List** property.

- List items can be removed using the **RemoveItem** method, and the selected item referenced by its **ListIndex** property.

11 Developing apps

This chapter demonstrates some advanced features used in the development of Excel apps with VBA macros.

Ignoring modes

UserForm custom dialogs are modal by default, so they must be closed before the user can continue working on a worksheet. When you prefer to display a UserForm that does allow the user to continue working on a worksheet, simply include the **vbModeless** constant after its **Show** method call.

A "modeless" UserForm can be useful to display and manipulate specific worksheet data or display additional information, such as images, relevant to the user's worksheet selections:

Modeless.xlsm

1 Add an **Image** control to a UserForm, then name that control as "imgPhoto" and the form as "frmViewer"

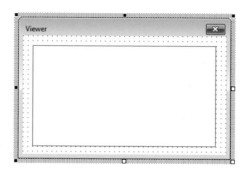

2 In Project Explorer, double-click the **ThisWorkbook** node

3 Select the **Workbook** item in the Editor's left-hand drop-down list, and the **SheetSelectionChange** item in its right-hand drop-down list – to add an event-handler code block
Private Sub Workbook_SheetSelectionChange _
(ByVal Sh As Object , ByVal Target As Range)

' Statements to be inserted here (Steps 4-7).

End Sub

4 Insert a statement to add error handling
On Error Resume Next

5 Next, insert three variable declarations
Dim make As String
Dim model As String
Dim path As String

Hot tip

Notice that this event-handler is passed two arguments – the worksheet in which a selection changed, and the current selection.

6 Now, insert statements to initialize each variable
```
make = Sh.Cells( Target.Row , 1 ).Value
model = Sh.Cells( Target.Row , 2 ).Value
path = ActiveWorkbook.path & _
   "\images\" & model & ".jpg"
```

7 Finally, insert statements to assign **Caption** and **Picture** property values to the UserForm
```
frmViewer.Caption = make & " " & model
frmViewer.imgPhoto.Picture = LoadPicture( path )
```

8 Insert a General code module into the project, and add a macro subroutine to display the UserForm and trigger the **Workbook_SheetSelectionChange( )** event-handler
```
Sub Viewer( )

frmViewer.Show vbModeless
Range( "A2" ).Select

End Sub
```

9 Add text to the worksheet and a button to run the macro, then open the UserForm and select rows – to see cell values appear on the title bar and to see a related image

Hot tip

ActiveWorkbook. path returns the system location of the Excel file. It is used here to build a path to a file in an adjacent "images" folder.

Hot tip

Notice how the **LoadPicture( )** function is used here to assign an image file to a control.

Don't forget

Each image filename exactly matches the text in the second column, plus each has a "**.jpg**" file extension.

Indicating progress

For macros that take a while to execute, it is useful to provide a progress indicator so the user understands that Excel is running the code. Typically, this is in the form of a graphical bar that expands and indicates the percentage of the task so far completed. This can be achieved using a Label control as the bar, and a Frame control caption to indicate the percentage:

ProgressBar.xlsm

1 Add a **Frame** control and a **Label** control to a **UserForm**

2 Name them "fraBar", "lblBar", and "frmProgress"

3 Click **View**, **Code** to open the form's code-behind page, then add this event-handler – to set the color and size of the Label control when the UserForm first opens
Private Sub UserForm_Initialize( )

lblBar.BackColor = vbRed
lblBar.Width = 0

End Sub

4 Next, on the code-behind page, add this subroutine – to expand the Label control and display the percentage of the task so far completed, as reported by an argument
Public Sub ReportProgress(perCent As Double)

lblBar.Width = perCent * (fraBar.Width - 10)
fraBar.Caption = Format(perCent , "0%")
Repaint

End Sub

Hot tip

The built-in **Format( )** function translates the argument to a percentage, and the **Repaint** method updates the visual appearance of the Label control.

5 Next, insert a General VBA code module into the project and add a subroutine that will fill cells with values
Sub FillCells( )

' Statements to be inserted here (Steps 6-9).

End Sub

6 Next, insert statements that declare four variables
```
Dim num As Integer
Dim row As Integer
Dim col As Integer
Dim perCent As Double
```

7 Now, insert statements to clear the worksheet and open the UserForm
```
ActiveSheet.Cells.Clear
frmProgress.Show vbModeless
```

Don't forget

The UserForm here is modeless, so the user could continue working on another worksheet while the loop executes.

8 Then, insert a nested loop to fill 5,000 cells with the loop counter value on each iteration
```
num = 1
For row = 1 To 500
  For col = 1 To 10
  ActiveSheet.Cells( row , col ) = num
  num = num + 1
  Next col

' Statements to be inserted here (Step 10).

Next row
```

9 Insert a statement to close the UserForm on completion
```
Unload frmProgress
```

Beware

To call the **Public** subroutine in the form's code module from the General VBA code module, you must prefix the subroutine name with the form name.

10 Insert statements to calculate and report the percentage of the task so far completed
```
perCent = num / 5000
frmProgress.ReportProgress( perCent )
```

11 Insert a button on the worksheet to run the macro and see the progress bar report as the cells get filled

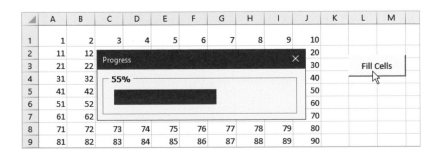

Controlling MultiPages

For custom dialogs that have many controls it is useful to provide tabs by placing a MultiPage control on the UserForm. Each group of controls can then be placed on a separate "page", so the user can recognize the individual steps of a process:

MultiPages.xlsm

1 Add a **MultiPage** control on the UserForm, then right-click a tab and choose **New Page** – to add a third tab

2 On the first page, add two **OptionButton** controls and name them "optThn" and "optDpp"

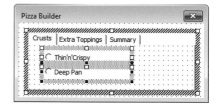

3 On the second page, add two **CheckBox** controls and name them "chkPep" and "chkMsh"

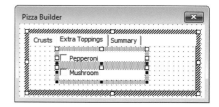

4 On the third page, add a **CommandButton** and **ListBox** and name them "cmdCan" and "lstSum"

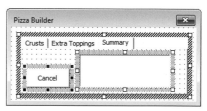

5 Edit the **Caption** property of each control as illustrated

6 Click **View, Code** to open the form's code-behind page, then add this subroutine to summarize the control states
Sub Summarize( )

lstSum.Clear

If optThn.Value = True Then lstSum.AddItem optThn.Caption
If optDpp.Value = True Then lstSum.AddItem optDpp.Caption
If chkPep.Value = True Then lstSum.AddItem chkPep.Caption
If chkMsh.Value = True Then lstSum.AddItem chkMsh.Caption

End Sub

Notice that the **If** test can be written on one line if **Then** is followed by a single statement or multiple colon-separated statements.

7 Next, add two event-handlers that respond when the user selects an **OptionButton** on the first page

```
Private Sub optThn_Click( )
Summarize
End Sub

Private Sub optDpp_Click( )
Summarize
End Sub
```

Double-click on a control in Design View to add its **Click** event-handler onto the code-behind page.

8 Now, add two event-handlers that respond when the user selects a **CheckBox** on the second page

```
Private Sub chkPep_Click( )
Summarize
End Sub

Private Sub chkMsh_Click( )
Summarize
End Sub
```

8 Finally, add an event-handler that resets all controls when the user pushes the **CommandButton** on the third page

```
Private Sub cmdCan_Click( )

lstSum.Clear
optThn.Value = False
optDpp.Value = False
chkPep.Value = False
chkMsh.Value = False

End Sub
```

A MultiPage object has a **Pages** property that is a zero-based array of its pages. This in turn has a **Controls** property that is a zero-based array of its controls. These can be used to reference any control on any page. For example, to reference the caption of the first OptionButton on the first page in this example: *MultiPageName.* **Pages(0).Controls(0). Caption**.

10 Run the macro, then make selections on the first two pages to see them summarized on the third page

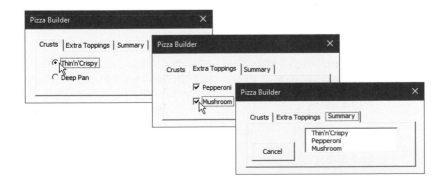

175

Tabbing data pages

In contrast to the MultiPage control that can provide different controls on each "page" (as demonstrated in the previous example), the TabStrip control provides the same controls on each page to display different data. Typically, the data displayed will be related, such as sales figures from different regions:

	A	B	C	D	E
1	Sales	Region 1	Region 2		
2	Target :	$75,000.00	$85,000.00		
3	Actual :	$68,000.00	$81,500.00		
4					

DataTabs.xlsm

1 Place a **TabStrip** control on a UserForm and see it has two tabs by default

2 Add descriptive labels plus two **TextBox** controls, a further **Label** control, and a **CommandButton** as below

3 Name the form "tabPrf" and the highlighted controls as "txtTgt", "txtSls", "lblPct", and "cmdUpdate" respectively

4 Click **View, Code** to open the form's code-behind page, then add this subroutine to populate the controls
Sub Populate( )

```
Select Case tabPrf.SelectedItem.Index
Case 0
txtTgt.Value = Range( "B2" ).Value
txtSls.Value = Range( "B3" ).Value
Case 1
txtTgt.Value = Range( "C2" ).Value
txtSls.Value = Range( "C3" ).Value
End Select
lblPct.Caption = Format( txtSls.Value / txtTgt.Value , "0%" )

End Sub
```

Hot tip

The tabs are a zero-based array so the current tab can be referenced by its **SelectedItem.Index** number.

5 Next, add an event-handler to caption the tabs

```
Private Sub UserForm_Initialize( )

    tabPrf.Tabs( 0 ).Caption = Range( "B1" ).Value
    tabPrf.Tabs( 1 ).Caption = Range( "C1" ).Value

End Sub
```

The Properties Window displays the TabStrip properties but does not have Caption properties for individual tabs – these can be set in code.

6 Now, add an event-handler to re-populate controls when the user selects a different tab

```
Private Sub tabPrf_Change( )
Populate
End Sub
```

7 Finally, add an event-handler to update the worksheet and form after the user changes a value in the form

```
Private Sub cmdUpdate_Click( )

    Select Case tabPrf.SelectedItem.Index
    Case 0
    Range( "B2" ).Value = txtTgt.Value
    Range( "B3" ).Value  = txtSls.Value
    Case 1
    Range( "C2" ).Value = txtTgt.Value
    Range( "C3" ).Value = txtSls.Value
    End Select
    lblPct.Caption = Format( txtSls.Value / txtTgt.Value , "0%" )

End Sub
```

To add more tabs, right-click on the TabStrip in Design View and select New Page. Each tab page will contain the same controls.

8 Add a button to the worksheet to run the macro, then use the UserForm tabs to manipulate the worksheet data

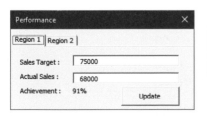
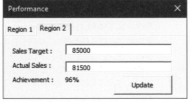
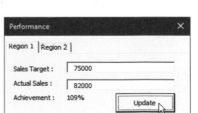

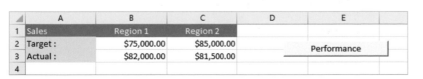

	A	B	C	D	E
1	Sales	Region 1	Region 2		
2	Target :	$75,000.00	$85,000.00		Performance
3	Actual :	$82,000.00	$81,500.00		
4					

177

Showing chart info

VBA does not provide a dedicated UserForm control for Excel charts, but you can export a chart as an image then display it in an Image control. Where the UserForm is modeless, the chart image can also be dynamically updated when the user changes data that is displayed in the chart:

ChartInfo.xlsm

1 Select some data on worksheet "Sheet1" and create an embedded chart of it, then move the chart to "Sheet2"

2 Add an **Image** control to a UserForm and rename it as "imgChart", then name the form "frmInfo"

3 Click **View**, **Code** to open the form's code-behind page, then add this Public subroutine that declares two variables
Public Sub LoadChart( )

Dim info As Chart
Dim path As String

' Statements to be inserted here (Steps 4-6).

End Sub

Hot tip

The **ChartObjects** are a collection of embedded chart objects.

4 Insert a statement to assign the chart object to a variable
Set info = Sheets("Sheet2").ChartObjects(1).Chart

5 Next, insert a statement to specify a filename to be located in a sub-folder named "images"
path = ActiveWorkbook.path & "\images\chart.jpg"

6 Now, insert statements to create an image file then display it on the UserForm
info.Export path
imgChart.LoadPicture(path)

Beware

The path expects there to be a folder named "images" alongside this Excel file.

7 Add an event-handler to display the chart image when the UserForm first opens
Private Sub UserForm_Initialize( )

LoadChart

End Sub

8 Double-click the Sheet1 node in Project Explorer, to open that code module, then add this event-handler to update the displayed chart image if the UserForm is open

Private Sub Worksheet_SelectionChange _
  (ByVal Target As Range)

  If Not frmInfo.Visible Then Exit Sub

  frmInfo.LoadChart

End Sub

9 Next, insert a VBA code module into the project and add a subroutine that will open the UserForm modelessly

Sub ChartInfo( )
frmInfo.Show vbModeless
End Sub

10 Add a button to the worksheet to run the macro and see the chart displayed

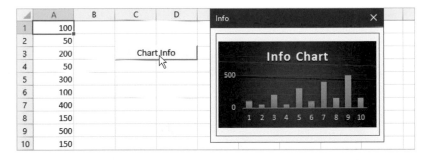

11 Change chart data on the worksheet, then hit **Enter** to see the chart displayed on the UserForm get dynamically updated

Creating Add-ins

If you have created an Excel VBA application for distribution, you can simply supply the workbook file or convert the application to an Excel "Add-in". Creating an Add-in provides a professional touch and allows you to password-protect your VBA code. With an Add-in, the workbook window is not visible to the user, but they can access the macro code to run the application:

QuickChart.xlsm

1 Produce and thoroughly test the application for bugs – in this case an app to quickly produce a simple chart from data contained in selected worksheet cells

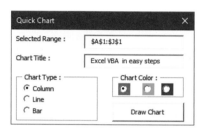

Beware

It will be much more difficult for the user to run a protected Excel Add-in if a shortcut key is not provided.

2 Click **Developer**, **Macros** and allocate shortcut keys if you wish to password-protect the app for distribution

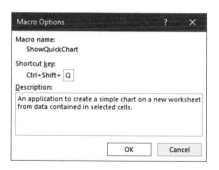

3 Open the Visual Basic Editor, then right-click the project node in Project Explorer and select **VBAProject Properties** from the context menu

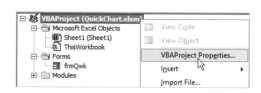

4 Select the **General** tab, then change the default project name to that of the app and enter a brief description of its purpose

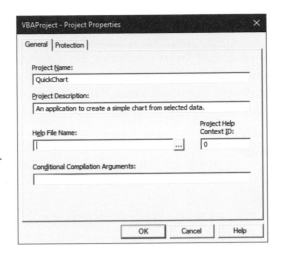

5 If you wish to password-protect the app, now select the **Protection** tab and check the "Lock project" box, then enter a password twice and click **OK**

Locking the project will prevent easy access but is not an absolute guarantee of protection.

6 Return to Excel, then click **File**, **Save As** and choose the **Excel Add-in (*.xlam)** file type from the drop-down list

7 Browse to your preferred location at which to create the file, then click **Save** to create the Excel Add-in

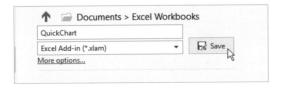

QuickChart.xlam

Typically, Excel suggests Add-ins are saved at **C:\Users*username*\\AppData\Roaming\\Microsoft\Addins** – but they can be saved anywhere.

Installing Add-ins

Having created an Add-in, on pages 180-181, it can be distributed to users for installation into their Excel application, together with instructions on its use. If the Add-in is password-protected, the users will not be able to view or edit the macro code unless the password is also provided. Installing the Add-in will allow the user to run the macro:

QuickData.xlsm

1 Launch Excel, then choose **File**, **Options** and select the **Adds-ins** item in the left-hand pane

2 In the **Manage** drop-down list at the bottom of the right-hand pane, select **Excel Add-ins**, then click the **Go** button – to launch the "Add-ins" dialog box

Hot tip

Some Add-ins are bundled with Excel and appear in the Add-ins dialog box, but are not installed unless you check their checkbox.

3 Click the **Browse...** button, then navigate to the location of the Add-in file and click the **OK** button to install it

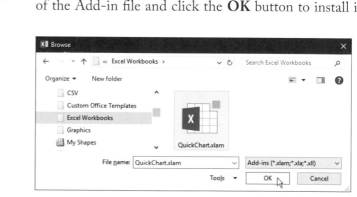

4 See the Excel Add-in get added to the **Add-ins** dialog list, with a check mark indicating it is now installed

Hot tip

You can uninstall an Add-in by renaming or deleting the **.xlam** file, then unchecking its box in the Add-ins dialog. You will then be asked if you want to delete it from the list.

5 Use the shortcut allocated to the Add-in to run the macro – in this example, press the **Ctrl + Shift + Q** keys

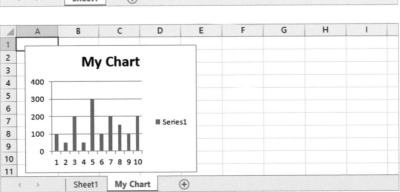

Don't forget

A shortcut must be allocated when you create the Add-in, for the user to run the macro – its worksheet is not accessible to the user.

183

Adding Ribbon buttons

When distributing an Add-in that is not locked with password-protection, the user can add a Ribbon button to execute the macro:

QuickData.xlsm

1 Launch Excel, then choose **File**, **Options** to launch the "Excel Options" dialog box, then select the **Customize Ribbon** item in the left-hand pane

2 In the "Choose commands from" drop-down list, select the **Macros** item to see the Add-in's macro command

The macro command will not appear in the list if the macro is locked with password protection, so the user cannot add a button for it in this way – they can use its shortcut keys instead.

3 Select the **Home** group in the right-hand pane, then click the **New Group** button

4 Click the **Rename** button and enter a group name of your choice in the "Rename" dialog – we chose "In Easy Steps"

5 Select the new group in the right-hand pane and the macro command in the center, then click the **Add** button – see the macro command added to the group in the right-hand pane

6 Select the macro command in the right-hand pane, then click the **Rename** button once more to re-open the dialog

7 Choose an appropriate button icon and edit the button's **Display name** to your preference

8 Click **OK** to close the "Rename" dialog box

9 Now, click **OK** to close the "Excel Options" dialog and see the button appear in its new group on the **Home** tab

You can return to the Rename dialog box to edit the display name or choose a different icon at any time.

10 Finally, push the button to run the macro

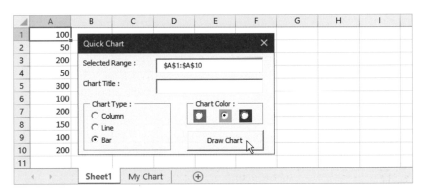

This macro is coded to choose its own chart title if the user leaves the TextBox empty once. This macro and all other examples in this book are available for download at **www.ineasysteps. com**/resource-centre/ downloads

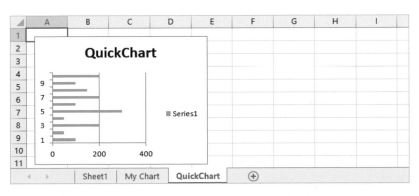

Summary

- Including the **vbModeless** constant when showing a **UserForm** lets the user continue working on a worksheet.

- A modeless **UserForm** can be useful to provide information relevant to the current worksheet selection.

- A **Label** control can visually indicate the progress of a task, and a **Frame** caption can numerically indicate its progress.

- The **Repaint** method can be used to update the visual appearance of a form control after it has changed.

- It is useful to provide **MultiPage** tabs for custom dialogs that have many controls.

- Each page of a **MultiPage** tab can provide different controls so the user can recognize individual steps of a process.

- Each page of a **TabStrip** control provides the same controls to display different related data.

- There is no control to directly display an Excel chart on a custom **UserForm** dialog.

- A chart can be exported as an image, then that image loaded into an **Image** control to display a chart on a custom dialog.

- A modeless **UserForm** displaying a chart image can be dynamically updated when the user changes data.

- An Excel VBA application can be distributed by sharing a copy of the workbook or by creating an **Add-in** version.

- Optionally, Excel **Add-in** files can be password-protected.

- An **Add-in** does not display the workbook to the user, but allows them access to macro code to run the application.

- A shortcut key should be allocated when creating an **Add-in** to provide a means for the user to run the macro.

- The user must install an **Add-in** into their Excel application before they can run its macro code.

- A button can be added to a custom group on the Excel **Ribbon** to run an **Add-in** that is not password-protected.

Index

W

X

Y